To the Heart of Asia

Sven Hedin, ca. 1930. (Photograph by D. Hummel.)

To the Heart of Asia

The Life of Sven Hedin

GEORGE KISH

Ann Arbor   The University of Michigan Press

Library of Congress Cataloging in Publication Data

Kish, George, 1914–
  To the heart of Asia.

  Bibliography: p.
  1. Hedin, Sven Anders, 1865–1952.   2. Explorers—
Sweden—Biography.   I. Title.
G306.H4K57   1984   910'.92'4 [B]   84-11850
ISBN 0-472-10056-4

To the memory of
Dr. David Hummel,
physician, scientist, humanitarian.
His enthusiastic support
made this book possible.

*It still happens that in my dreams I hear the
melancholy sound of the caravans' bronze bells, that
song of the deserts, unchanged through thousands of years. . . .*

Preface to *Great Men and Kings*

Preface

Sven Hedin was an explorer, a man eager to see unknown places, to name unnamed mountains, to fill in those white areas on the map labeled "unexplored."

What makes an explorer? Hedin gave the answer to that question when he described the event that made him decide, at the age of fifteen, to spend his life in pursuit of the unknown and to gain fame and fortune.

It was on April 24, 1880, that a Swedish geologist, Adolf Erik Nordenskiöld, returned aboard his ship *Vega* from a voyage that caught the imagination of the whole world and swept all of Sweden into a frenzy of excitement and pride. *Vega,* manned and staffed almost entirely by Swedes, was the first ship to sail from Europe past the shores of Siberia to the Pacific, along the fabled and long-sought Northeast Passage. From Bering Strait, the tiny vessel sailed around Asia and Europe, and at ten o'clock that cold, rainy April evening it came to anchor in Stockholm's inner harbor, in front of the royal palace.

Sven Hedin's father packed his family into a carriage, drove through the long, crowded streets of Stockholm, and stopped on a low hill overlooking the harbor to watch *Vega*'s triumphal homecoming. Sven Hedin sat on the box with the coachman. He remembered every detail of that scene for the rest of his life: the roar of the crowds, the fireworks, the searchlights picking out the tiny ship as it came to a stop in the harbor. It was like a Roman triumph, he wrote later.

It was indeed a triumph for Nordenskiöld. He was created a baron of the realm by King Oscar II and honored throughout Europe. His book on the voyage of the *Vega* became a best-seller that was translated into many languages. These were achievements worth striving for, and that evening Hedin knew that he was going to be an explorer.

Sven Hedin did achieve fame and fortune. As a reward for his explorations in Asia, he was elevated to the nobility, the last Swede to achieve that distinction. On his return from one of his voyages in Asia, he too was received with enthusiasm in Stockholm. His books, translated into many languages, made his name known throughout the world. He was honored by kings and emperors and by the great geographical societies of the world.

Yet Hedin was never fully satisfied with the rewards of his career as an explorer. Nor did he get full satisfaction from being a very much sought-after public speaker and popular lecturer. He was always fascinated with politics, with foreign affairs, with military matters. He became involved in several of the great political debates of his time in Sweden; later in life he thought of himself as an elder statesman of all Scandinavia.

But the world of politics is not a simple one where achievements can be readily measured, known against unknown, discovery against lack of knowledge. Hedin had to learn that the rewards in politics are not lasting, that open commitments to a cause can bring disappointment, grief, even disgrace. Because he always supported Germany regardless of its form of government, after the Second World War he was ignored by many of his countrymen and scorned by others.

Little of that disappointment is reflected in the voluminous diary Hedin kept during the last twenty-two years of his life. His own views never changed; he continued to regard the world in the same way he had in his youth, during the 1880s and 1890s: Russia was evil, lurking across the Baltic, waiting for a chance to bring Sweden, Scandinavia, and even all of Europe under its tyrannical rule. England was the very symbol of imperialism, defending its ill-gotten gains at all costs, ready to sacrifice others to preserve the Empire. Germany, in contrast, was the shining hope of mankind, the chosen leader of the Germanic peoples, including all Scandinavians. When set against the realities of its time, Hedin's worldview was often anachronistic.

However, Hedin is remembered not for his political activities but for the achievements of his travels in Asia. The scientific results he and other men under his leadership obtained are his lasting monument. Hedin was not only a fine geographer, a map-maker of extraordinary talent, and an artist of unusual skill; he was also a master of the art of public relations. He made explora-tion exciting, and through his books and public lectures geogra-phy achieved a popular appeal that few others had been able to give it.

Sven Hedin believed in what he was doing and made certain that a full record of it was kept. He wrote voluminously and carried on a worldwide correspondence throughout his long life. His published writings, his letters, and his diary cover most as-pects of his career. They provided most of the facts related in his book.

To round out this portrait of an explorer, I was fortunate to have met and listened to Hedin's companions on his last expedi-tion to Inner Asia: Dr. David Hummel, professors Erik Norin and Birger Bohlin, and Dr. Waldemar Haude. Hedin's grandnephew and his grandnieces offered precious insights into his daily life. His friends and associates in Sweden and Germany shared their memories of him.

I was also fortunate to have had access to Hedin's own archives, kept in the National Archives of Sweden, through permission from the Sven Hedin Foundation in Stockholm. Frau Suzanne Brockhaus, whose father-in-law and husband were Hedin's Ger-man publishers and close friends for over sixty years, opened the archives of the publishing house of F. A. Brockhaus for me.

This book owes its inception to my good friend Wilhelm Odel-berg and its completion to the generous financial support given by Dr. David Hummel, the members of the Hedin family, and the Hedin Foundation. The Faculty Research Fund, Horace H. Rack-ham School of Graduate Studies, University of Michigan, pro-vided support for publication. Without their assistance the task of drawing a portrait of Sven Hedin would have been impossible.

Ann Arbor, at the House of the Seven Plum Trees

Contents

I

Growing Up in Stockholm

Sven Anders Hedin was born in Stockholm on February 19, 1865, the second child and older son of Ludvig and Anna Hedin. His father's people traced the family back to the mid-1600s, when the first man to bear the name, Lars Hedin, was an official in a small town west of Stockholm. Lars Hedin's father was a farmer, known only by his first name, but Lars's children climbed rapidly to middle-class respectability. His son was a Lutheran minister and his grandson a civil servant; his great-grandson, the first Sven Anders Hedin, studied under the great naturalist Linnaeus at Uppsala University, took his medical degree, and became personal physician to King Gustav III of Sweden.

The family's standing was well established when Sven Hedin's grandfather married the daughter of one of Stockholm's wealthiest citizens, Abraham W. Westman, known as "the king of brewers." But the family fortunes took a bad turn when both of Hedin's grandparents died in the same year and left nine children alone and penniless. Thus it was that Hedin's father, Ludvig, first learned the mason's trade. He later put himself through art school and qualified as an architect. He had talent and ambition and, when still a young man, was appointed city architect of Stockholm—a post of honor and substance.

When Sven Hedin was born, the Hedin family was well known and well liked in Stockholm. Two of his uncles held good civil service jobs, but it was the third, Svante Hedin, who was the best-known member of the family. He was one of the most popular actors of his time.

The Hedin family was respectable. It also had an artistic and a scholarly tradition. The family, though not of the court aristocracy, also had long-standing ties to the royal house of Sweden. King Gustav III stood godfather to Hedin's grandmother. His uncle Svante, the actor, was a boon companion to King Carl XV. In later years, this royal connection was to stand Hedin in good stead, giving him not only prestige but also strong support, both financial and moral, for his travels.

Hedin's maternal grandfather, Christian Gissel Berlin, started his career as a mathematician, turned later to theology, achieved high rank in the state church of Sweden, and played a role in the Swedish parliament as well. Yet he was the grandson of an immigrant, a Jewish rabbi who came to Sweden in 1770. Abraham Brode, Hedin's maternal ancestor, was born in Prussia, became a rabbi, and held posts with congregations in his native Germany. He first visited Sweden as a member of the suite of Prince Henry of Prussia. He liked the country so well that he returned in 1771 to Malmö, in southernmost Sweden, and was baptized under the name of Johan Christian Berlin. He tried his luck as a businessman but failed, and nothing is known of his later life. The children from his marriage with a Swedish woman did well, however; they achieved success in the Lutheran church and in the service of the Swedish state and were fully accepted by their fellows of the Swedish middle class.

Were it not for Sven Hedin's strongly expressed support for the National Socialist government of Hitler, well known for its anti-Semitic policies, the whole matter of his ancestry would interest only the student of family trees. Hedin himself never denied his Jewish ancestry. In 1937, when anti-Jewish legislation was well underway in Germany, Hedin wrote:

Every sixteenth drop of my blood is of Jewish origin. I insist on that one-sixteenth and will not lose it. It comes from a people who lived through thousands of years of ill fortune and have ridden out worse storms than any other people on earth. It may have been that one-sixteenth of my blood that helped me in moments of despair and was to my advantage in dealing with the peoples of the East. (1937, 276)

Ludvig and Anna Hedin had seven children, five daughters and two sons. The parents themselves lived long and useful lives. Hedin's father died at ninety-one, his mother at eighty-seven. Theirs was a warm and affectionate family, with ties so strong that only one of their children married. Through their own long lives (they all lived well past seventy) the Hedin brothers and sisters lived together and acted as a close-knit family group.

Religion played an important part in the family. Daily prayers were said before meals, and everybody prayed at night; Hedin followed this custom wherever he was, in the deserts and mountains of Inner Asia, in an industrialist's mansion in Chicago. Another family custom was the reading of a Bible verse every evening, from the collection of *Dagenslösen* (The Lord's word for the day), published by the Moravian Brethren. Hedin took a copy with him on all his travels, and as he read the verse for the day, he felt secure in the knowledge that thousands of miles away, his beloved family was about to read it, too. The thought gave him comfort and strength.

Ludvig and Anna Hedin taught their children responsibility for their own lives and respect for work. And they all worked, each at his or her task, as best they could. Clara, the oldest, ran a stationery shop for many years in downtown Stockholm, in partnership with one of her cousins. Emma acted most of the time as the general manager of the household. Alma, the youngest of the children, had her own career as a social worker and was one of the first women members of Stockholm's City Council. But as the years went on, Sven, the famous member of the family, became the central figure. After his retirement, Ludvig Hedin acted as his son's unpaid and very efficient secretary, copying in his own clear hand his son's manuscripts for publication.

After his father died, it was Hedin's brother and sisters who looked after his accounts, typed the letters he wrote longhand, and copied manuscripts to be sent to the printer. No one could have had a more devoted staff. In another very real way, the close ties that bound the Hedin family together made many of Hedin's books, especially his popular travel books, possible. From his first voyage onward, he followed the habit of writing long letters to the family, letters that took the place of a diary and dealt with people and places. Back home, these letters were carefully filed in chronological order, and when Hedin returned from a voyage he could go back to them, using them as reminders of specific events and including substantial sections from them in his narrative. Only in this way was he able to write as speedily and as voluminously as he did throughout his life.

In Sweden, children started school at the age of seven, and after elementary school Hedin attended the best private high school in all Stockholm, known then and now as the Beskow School, after its founder and principal. He was not the best of students and did not complete secondary school until the age of twenty. But he had many outside interests, chief among them drawing, especially drawing maps. He did inherit his father's graphic skill as well as his energy and inner drive. While still in his teens, he compiled a six-volume set of hand-drawn maps dealing with the physical world, but first and foremost, in a separate volume, he dealt with the Arctic. The maps remained in manuscript form and were never published.

The fact that young Hedin was a skilled mapmaker was well known to his father's friends, and one day he was asked to draw a map of Central Asia that would be used in a lecture on the discoveries of the distinguished Russian explorer Przhevalsky. It was a huge map, too big to be drawn on the dining room table at the Hedins' apartment where young Sven had worked before: he had to draw it at the Stockholm Art School. When the map was displayed during the lecture, which was given at a meeting of the Swedish Geographical Society, Hedin received high praise from his hero, Adolf Nordenskiöld.

At this time, Hedin was still very much influenced by Nordenskiöld's travels in the Arctic and wanted to follow in his footsteps. But in his last year in high school, something happened that changed his outlook and his whole life. The school principal asked him whether after graduation he would be willing to travel to the Russian city of Baku, on the Caspian Sea, and spend a year tutoring a young Swedish boy. Without a moment's hesitation Hedin replied, "Of course, I shall be glad to go." The die was thus cast, and at twenty years of age he began his travels in Asia, not in the Arctic.

The offer to Hedin came from a Swedish engineer, Sandgren, who was working for the Nobel brothers in the Baku oil fields and wanted his son to be ready to enter Swedish schools when they returned home. Hedin was offered his traveling expenses and a modest salary for eight months of teaching.

It was the biggest moment thus far in the life of the Hedin family. They had always led a sedentary life, never traveling further than to the islands surrounding Stockholm for a short summer vacation. Here was Sven, ready to cross all of Russia to the very borders of Asia. Preparations were made and on August 15, 1885, the family assembled in their living room. Father Hedin read from the Bible and recited the Lord's Prayer. Then they all went down to the harbor—parents, five daughters, a son, and three uncles—to see Sven board a steamer to Finland, on his way to Russia.

As the ship sailed through the islands that separate Stockholm from the Baltic, Sven sat on deck, even though it was raining, bidding goodbye to his homeland. But he was not alone, for at many points along the way, friends of the family who had cottages in the vicinity assembled outside to shout and wave to the young man beginning a long voyage. As Hedin wrote home later, the other passengers wondered who he was to have so many friends (August 18, 1885).

Sven Hedin was on his way—to Baku, to the Caspian Sea, to Asia.

II

Introduction to Asia, 1884–85

Sven Hedin had never traveled more than a hundred kilometers from his home in Stockholm; now he was on the first leg of a trip of more than two thousand five hundred kilometers, crossing all of Russia. He had only a few short hours to spend in the capital of the Russian Empire, Saint Petersburg, before getting on the train to his first stop, Moscow. In his letter home, he described the Kremlin as

> a chaos of bizarre buildings, having crenellated walls with openings for cannon, towers ornamented with pictures of saints and paintings in all the colors of the rainbow, gilded cupolas that shine in the burning hot sun. From a distance the cupolas burn like diamonds, while others are blue, green, yellow. And on Red Square, in front of the Kremlin, stands the church of St. Basil, with its indescribable wealth of color. (August 20, 1885)

From Moscow to the Caucasus it was a four-day journey by train, tedious at times, but constantly offering new impressions of people and buildings. Hedin had a sketchbook with him, and drew the first of thousands of sketches that became a distinct and delightful feature of his books. He had inherited his father's artistic skill, but as he put it, had had but a few weeks instruction in drawing one summer while he was still in high school (1920, 6). He worked with a lead pencil and sometimes with pen and ink and by his own admission preferred sketching to taking photographs. He sketched people standing on the platform of railroad stations, merchants in their stalls in bazaars, and monuments that impressed him. To draw was a joy, and became an important part of his life.

> Each picture is a memory of a day in Asia and therefore part of my life. Each drawing reminds me not only of a particular episode from that journey, it unfolds a whole chain of events of which it was only a single link. To look at a sketch gives color to the setting, and life and movement to men and beasts. I see a caravan marching between sand dunes, I hear the echo of horses' hooves across mountains. . . . I never forget a landscape I had sketched. Why, I sat right there and paid it full attention, and I remember every detail of that moment, what time of the year it was, was I chilled to the bone or not, was the mood of the caravan good or were we worried, did we have enough supplies or were we short on food, whence we came and where we went. My sketches are like seven-mile boots that help me retrace my steps, day by day, through the long years in Asia. (1920, 169–70)

The first part of the journey came to an end at the town of Vladikavkaz (now called Ordzhonikidze), in the northern foothills of the mighty Caucasus mountains. To reach Baku, travelers had to cross the Caucasus by a road built by the Russians to connect the northern and southern parts of the range. To this day it remains the only all-weather road across the Caucasus, and it is still called the Georgian Military Road; it leads to the region called Georgia and ends at the Georgian capital of Tiflis (now called Tbilisi). It was a journey of twenty-eight hours by stagecoach, and Hedin had occasion to marvel at the scenery. "The dark shadows had already fallen on the mountainsides, while the peaks were still shining with a blinding, silvery light, as if they had been illuminated with searchlights" (August 20, 1885).

From Tiflis, the journey continued by train once more to the city of Baku, then the oil capital of Russia on the shore of the Caspian Sea. At that time the Baku oil fields were the world's largest; the Nobel brothers, who controlled many of the wells, laid the foundations of their family fortune there. Hedin's employer,

Sandgren, lived in the town of Balakani, surrounded by the derricks and pumps of the oil field.

From late August, 1885, until April, 1886, Sven Hedin stayed with the Sandgrens, tutoring their older son, Erhard. He spent his free time visiting as much of the area around Baku as possible, sketching, watching the people: Tatars, Turks, Georgians, Russians. Being of a careful nature, he did not discard the white, visored cap that he had worn for his high school graduation (a custom that is still observed in Sweden). He wrote to his family that people were curious about his cap, that several of them asked what it meant, and that many believed that he held an important rank in the Swedish Army. That mistake is easy to explain, since the summer uniform of officers in the tsar's army did indeed include a white, visored cap.

But above all else, Hedin spent his free time learning languages. He already knew enough German and French to make himself understood. Now he launched himself headlong into learning something about the languages of Asia. In February, 1886, he wrote home:

> On some days I used the following languages, one after another: Latin and French with Erhard [his pupil]; lessons in German and Persian by myself; Russian with my teacher; English with Mr. Sandgren; teaching Swedish to Bakhi Khanov [a young Tatar friend], and learning Turkish from him. Eight languages in one day! (February 3, 1886)

His skill in learning languages became one of Hedin's greatest assets. His command of German, French, English, and Russian was such that he could present formal lectures in each of them and elicit eloquent tributes to his fluency. Equally useful in his travels was his ability to converse in Turkish and Persian, and to these Oriental languages he later added Mongolian and Tibetan. Thus equipped, he was as much at home in the felt tent of a Mongol shepherd as in an elegant European drawing room.

At the beginning of 1886, Hedin suddenly became very ill. The local doctor diagnosed rheumatic fever and took very good care of his young patient. Hedin recovered quickly from his illness, one of the very few he experienced in his life, and more than sixty years later, he paid tribute to the man who he believed had saved his life.

> I shall never forget the thanks I owe to the old Polish Jew, Doctor Goritskii, who looked after me for a whole month with unfailing kindness, when I had a violent attack of rheumatic fever. . . . When I wanted to pay him for his services, he said, "I do not need your money, give it to the poor." He was indeed among the chosen few of mankind. (1950, 1:8)

By March, young Sandgren had completed all the work he was required to do for admission to a high school in Sweden. Hedin's assignment was finished, but he was not ready to return to Stockholm. Baku had its points of interest, but Asia, with all the mystery that word meant to the young Swede, was only a step away, beyond the Russian border.

Turkey was near, but Hedin had no interest in a trip to that country. Though by the 1880s its European territories were for the most part lost, to Hedin and his contemporaries Turkey was not really part of Asia. After all, Turkey was called the sick man of Europe; it was weak and exposed to its aggressive neighbors, the object of recurring revolutions and wars. But Persia, southeast of Baku, was another story. It was considered very much part of the Orient, and to a Swede it sounded exciting and mysterious. The question in Hedin's mind was not what the goal of his voyage should be, but how to make his dream come true.

He had saved a little money from his tutor's salary—then the equivalent of fifty U.S. dollars and worth probably ten times that much in today's terms, but still not a great deal. His father, to whom Hedin had written for help, sent him double that amount. Equally valuable to him was a letter of introduction to a Swedish dentist practicing in Tehran, the capital of Persia; Dr. Hybennet was also the personal dentist of the Shah. The letter was written by the most famous Swede of the time, the great Arctic explorer Nordenskiöld, and Hedin hoped that it would open doors for him in Persia. For the rest, he trusted his luck.

He left Baku on April 6, 1886, on a Russian steamer bound for the Persian port of Enseli on the Caspian. Back at home, his family was very worried. True, Baku was far from Stockholm, but it was in Russia, and to Swedes Russia was a next-door neighbor. There were railroads in Russia, daily newspapers, good mail service. Many Swedes found good jobs there as engineers, businessmen, and entrepreneurs. But Sven was going beyond the boundaries of Russia, into the vast continent of Asia.

Their worries were unnecessary. In those years of peace, the 1880s, Europe ruled the world, and Europeans were looked upon as a superior breed. That statement held true whatever the European's nationality may have been. Moreover, there was still a solidarity among Europeans whenever they met in other parts of the world. Russians, Englishmen, Germans, Frenchmen, Swedes may have had their differences at home, but far away, among "natives" of other continents, they tended to be friendly toward each other.

Europe ruled the world and in fact ruled Asia. Much of the continent was dominated by Britain and Russia, and while the Chinese Empire in the east and the Turkish Empire in the west loomed large on the map, they both had been reduced to complete impotence in international affairs. To be a European was a safe-conduct anywhere in Asia.

There was also an institution of crucial importance in Persia that Hedin may not have known about, but that was to be of great help to him on his journey—the overland telegraph. Built by Englishmen to connect London with its Indian empire, it ran across Europe and Turkey to Tehran and thence all the way to Calcutta. A branch line connected Tehran with the Persian Gulf. Stations along the line had European managers who made it their business to look after fellow Europeans who turned up in their territory. And Hedin was recommended to the staff of the telegraph company by his host in Tehran, Dr. Hybennet, the Swedish dentist.

The equipment Hedin started with on a journey of nearly 3,000 kilometers was light: he wore a camel hair suit and carried another with him together with underclothes and a heavy blanket. In a leather case that he slung over his shoulder he had a revolver, notebooks, and sketchbooks, and maps of Persia (1887,

48). En route from the Caspian to Tehran, riding on horseback, he stopped at the city of Rasht and paid a courtesy call on the Russian consul. This was his first encounter with the friendly and helpful manner of Europeans toward their fellows abroad; the consul not only wined and dined him but gave him a warm sleeping bag for his journey (April 19, 1886).

When his young countryman arrived in Tehran, Dr. Hybennet greeted him with open arms, showed him the sights, gave him good advice for his trip, and recommended that he use the Persian post system. The government of Persia maintained stations along the main roads radiating from Tehran where the traveler could rest, have a meal of sorts, and get a fresh horse for the next leg of the journey. The charge for horse and groom—the groom traveled along to bring the horse back to its permanent station—was modest, and so was the cost of accommodations. Travelers stayed in ancient hostels, called caravansaries, carrying their own bedding and purchasing whatever food was available. Hedin was young, with few demands, and managed to get along. He wrote home:

> When reaching a post station having ridden ten or more hours, you are desperately tired. You get bread, eggs, tea, the usual menu, from the nearest farm. After supper, you spread the saddle cover on the ground in one of the rooms of the hostel, put your sleeping bag and overcoat on top of you, use the saddle for a pillow, and you sleep so well that only the sunrise will waken you. (May 20, 1886)

As he rode south from Tehran, Hedin stopped to see the sights: the great square in Esfahan, the ancient capital of Persia, and the bazaar with its crowds of people, camels, and donkeys; the ruins of the palaces of Persepolis, once the heart of the Persian Empire that had stretched from the Mediterranean to the Indian Ocean in the fifth century B.C.; the gardens of Shiraz. As May wore on, the days got hotter and hotter, until the temperature rose to thirty-nine degrees Celsius in the shade. Finally, on May 22, he saw the sun rise above the mirrorlike waters of the Persian Gulf. In the distance he could distinguish the white houses of the port of Bushire. He had completed the first part of his journey, having ridden 1,500 kilometers in twenty-nine days. It was quite an accomplishment, especially for a man who had never ridden a horse before his arrival in Baku, and he felt satisfied.

Continuing his voyage, he took a steamer from Bushire to the port of Basra, on the Shatt-al-Arab, the stream formed by the junction of the great rivers Euphrates and Tigris. Basra was the busiest port of the Persian Gulf, and to read Hedin's description of its trade in the 1880s is to realize how little has changed there for centuries.

> To and through Basra come silk, linen, clothes, gold, silver, sandalwood, and indigo from India, pearls from Bahrain, coffee from Arabia, shawls and fruit from Persia, spices from Java. . . . Of those articles exported from Basra, dates are by far the most important. . . . The local Arabs say that in Basra alone there are seventy kinds of date palms, and according to a Persian poet the fruit of the date palm can be used in three hundred and sixty-three different ways. (1887, 224)

When he planned his trip, Hedin looked at the map and decided to go as far as Baghdad, a city he felt would offer him insights into the very heart of the East. It had been the seat of Arab emperors; its glamour was part of its existence. But when he arrived there, still traveling in modern ways, by river steamer, he found a busy and uninteresting town and after a very brief stay decided to return to Tehran.

Not only had Baghdad proved to be a disappointment, but his money was running out, and he could no longer travel on his own. The only way he could afford to go was to join a caravan bound for Tehran. Several Arab merchants, a Christian from Baghdad, and a few Moslem pilgrims returning to Persia made up the group accompanying some fifty mules carrying cloth and hardware from England to Persian markets. It was Hedin's first encounter with a caravan, and one he always remembered. It was June by this time; the days were too hot for travel, and the caravan moved by night, the stillness broken only by the drivers' shouts and the ringing of the bells worn by the beasts of burden. Sixty years later, he wrote of the sound of the caravan: "It still happens that in my dreams I hear the melancholy sound of the caravans' bronze bells, that song of the deserts, unchanged through thousands of years" (1950, 1:9).

The caravan moved too slowly to suit the mood of an impatient young man, and he also had trouble with his horse. On the third day out of Baghdad, one of the owners of the caravan caught up with it, riding a handsome white Arab stallion. Hedin knew that he had very little money left, but the temptation to ride this magnificent horse was too great. He spent all he had on hiring the horse for the first part of his return journey, across the mountains that separate Iraq from Persia to the Persian city of Kirmanshah. Once there, he found himself without a cent and several hundred kilometers from his destination, Tehran.

Others might have sold their saddles and their clothes, but Hedin had a different attitude. He was a European, after all, a man of the world, and someone was bound to help him, if he could only find the right person. His luck held. He remembered a conversation with the head of the Persian telegraph system, a German engineer named Houtum-Schindler, who had suggested that Hedin call on the British consular agent in Kirmanshah, Aga Muhammed Hassan, a wealthy merchant. Hedin's knowledge of the two languages of the area, Turkish and Persian, was crucial. He presented himself at the merchant's house, was admitted right away simply because he was a European, and could converse with Aga Hassan without needing an interpreter.

The Kirmanshah merchant asked Hedin where his home was. Sweden was unknown to Aga Hassan, but he had read Voltaire's biography of the warrior king Charles XII translated into Turkish, and being a countryman of Charles XII was all the introduction Hedin needed. He was treated as a visitor of high rank, dined with his host and notables of the city, saw the sights, and as a parting gift from his host was given a purse full of silver coins. To Hedin it must have seemed like a tale from the *Arabian Nights*, even though he found out afterward that the money was only a loan. Aga Muhammed Hassan sent a bill for that amount to

Hedin's friend in Tehran, Dr. Hybennet, who paid it in full (Letter from Houtum-Schindler, August 24, 1887).

The last leg of his trip was the hardest: he rode the five hundred kilometers from Kirmanshah to Tehran, across the rugged mountains and wide empty spaces of western Persia, with the postal courier. It was a fast ride, for the courier made only the briefest of stops, a few hours at most, and the last two days they rode without any rest, stopping only to change horses and have a quick meal of tea, bread, and fruit. He arrived at Dr. Hybennet's house in Tehran in torn and tattered clothes and once more without a penny, having given what little he had left to the courier.

After a hot bath and twenty-four hours' rest, he felt well enough to sum up his impressions in a letter home. His satisfaction with his accomplishment was evident.

> I travelled three thousand kilometers over deserts, snow-covered mountains, across rivers and streams, alone. I rode sixty horses, on dangerous roads, often in a wild manner, without being robbed; I travelled in unhealthy places without getting sick, in the brightest sunlight without getting a sunstroke. I rode horseback through pitch dark nights and fell asleep in the saddle without falling off and breaking my neck. I crossed swollen rivers without the horse losing its footing and me being carried off to drown. I even managed to ride a beautiful horse when I was out of funds. I fought Arabs and Turkish soldiers and came away unharmed and without having to draw my gun. (June 23, 1886)

There are obvious overstatements in this proud letter. But Sven Hedin felt that he had put himself to the test and passed with flying colors. The nature of the test appears obscure, but to him it seems to have meant facing a world different from the safe surroundings he had always known and having to use his own resources to meet emergencies. It was not a severe test, but it served an important purpose. Hedin had his first encounter with Asia and came away convinced that the way to glory and success was through exploration. He did not explore unknown lands this time, nor did he fill gaps in the map. That he would do the next time around.

After a few days in Tehran, the good Dr. Hybennet must once more have come to his young friend's rescue, though Hedin does not speak of it. He started on his way home, obviously provided with funds. He collected his belongings in Baku, visited Constantinople, and made a special stop in Budapest, Hungary.

Throughout his life, Hedin was a man who planned ahead carefully. This time, even though he had not even entered the university and possessed only a high school diploma, he planned to write a book on his trip across Persia. The best way to convince a publisher that his manuscript was worth being printed was to ask someone of great distinction to write a preface, rather than to risk being turned away as a young and unknown writer. That was precisely what Hedin had in mind. In Budapest he called on one of the great Orientalists of the time, Arminius Vámbéry, a Hungarian scholar.

Vámbéry was very much impressed with his young Swedish visitor, who managed to bring into the conversation his having found Vámbéry's signature on the wall of the grave of King Cyrus of Persia. He consented to write a preface to *Across Persia, Mesopotamia, and the Caucasus: Travel Memories*. Early in 1887, using the long letters he wrote home as a travel diary and digging deep into published material on Persia for additional information (all duly noted), Sven Hedin presented himself at the office of Albert Bonnier, Sweden's most prestigious publisher. Having the preface of the great Vámbéry did help, and a few months later a well-illustrated, handsome book of 460 pages appeared in the bookstores. It was favorably reviewed, and the young author received 2,500 Swedish kronor (500 dollars) as his honorarium.

While his classmates enrolled at the university or entered business, Sven Hedin had taken what at first must have seemed like a year's leave. The journey to Persia did not produce any new insights, nor did it create a stir among geographers. But to Hedin it served as an introduction to another world, a stengthening of his belief that being an explorer was a dream worthy of pursuing. He was ready to prepare himself for that career.

III

Student Days in Berlin, 1889–90

In the fall of 1886, Sven Hedin enrolled at the University of Stockholm. He had hoped to study geography, but the subject was taught neither at Stockholm nor at the much older and more prestigious Swedish universities of Uppsala and Lund. He had to settle for studies in geology, a discipline closely related to geography and considered one of its foundations. The lecturer in that subject was a Norwegian, Brøgger, who was full of enthusiasm for his subject and inspired his students both in the classroom and, during the spring vacation, on field trips to Norway.

Having completed the course in geology at Stockholm, Hedin took his final examinations at nearby Uppsala University, and in the fall of 1888 he became a "candidate in philosophy," the first degree in Swedish universities. It was time to plan for further study specializing in geography, but Hedin felt that there was another project that he wanted to finish first, another book that would strengthen his position when he enrolled as a post-graduate student. The project was ambitious: the translation, in abridged form, of the travels in Central Asia of the distinguished Russian explorer Colonel Nikolai Przhevalsky.

Przhevalsky had become known for his exploration of Chinese Central Asia and was considered one of the leading authorities on the geography of that vast, remote, and little-known area. Hedin was becoming more and more interested in Central Asia and hoped to learn more about it by preparing the translation. He persuaded the great explorer Nordenskiöld to write a preface, and Bonnier accepted it for publication.

All was going well until, in June, 1889, Hedin became ill with a serious eye infection. It was an inflammation of the iris, and for a short time there was even concern about his losing sight in one

17

eye. He recovered by the end of the summer but retained only limited vision in his left eye, and afterwards he had to depend on only one eye for all of his reading, writing, and drawing.

Early in September, the Hedin family rented a small cottage outside Stockholm where Hedin was to rest and get his strength back. He left the cottage only to attend the International Congress of Orientalists in the city. Many took notice of the young Swede who could converse with the scholars at the congress not only in English, German, and French, but in Turkish and Persian as well.

Hedin's skill as a linguist was brought to the attention of men high in government. During the congress, the delegation from Persia had presented to King Oscar II of Sweden the highest decoration the shah could bestow, and the gesture called for an appropriate acknowledgment. It was decided that a special mission should be sent to Tehran to return the favor by presenting to the shah Sweden's highest decoration, the Order of the Seraphim. The prime minister of Sweden, Baron Åkerhielm, knew Ludvig Hedin well, and when he heard that his friend's son spoke Persian, he decided that Sven should be a member of the mission to the shah.

Ludvig Hedin wrote to his son in late September, 1889, to tell him that he was to appear at the prime minister's office at ten o'clock the next morning. Sven got up before dawn, took the steamboat serving the resort to the city, and hurried to his parents' apartment. Father Hedin believed that a young man who was to wait on the prime minister must wear tails. Tails it was, and young Hedin presented himself at the prime minister's office in full evening dress.

Baron Åkerhielm looked him over carefully.

"You are going to a dinner?"
"No, your Excellency, not to-day."
"Is it for my sake that you are wearing tails?"
"Yes, your Excellency."
"This is totally unnecessary. I am a simple man, and I am not impressed by tails. I prefer a morning coat on a weekday like today."

Hedin thought he had committed a serious error, but things were in order. The prime minister introduced him to the minister for foreign affairs, and he was told that he would be a member of the mission to Persia as a *dragoman,* or interpreter, with the temporary rank of consul, so that he could wear a diplomat's uniform. Further details, including the date when the mission was to leave for Persia, were to be settled later (1950, 1:113–14).

The fact that he did not have to get ready for a trip to Persia right away suited Hedin. He had been planning to continue his education as a geographer abroad, and the schedule suggested by the minister for foreign affairs gave him a chance to do so.

In the 1890s, Germany led the world in the field of geographical research and teaching. Hedin's hero, Adolf Nordenskiöld, did post-graduate studies at the University of Berlin, and that was the university Hedin hoped to attend.

There was another reason for his choice. The principal chair of geography at the University of Berlin was held by Ferdinand von Richthofen, one of the leading scholars of the time. Richthofen's reputation rested largely on the pioneer work he wrote on the geography of China, based on his extensive travels in the Celestial Empire. Hedin wanted to learn as much as possible about Chinese Central Asia and Tibet, and Richthofen was the greatest authority on that subject. Armed with a letter of introduction from Nordenskiöld, Hedin went to Berlin and called on Professor Richthofen at his home.

Senior professors in German universities were regarded as demigods by their students. Richthofen's worldwide reputation made Hedin even more awestruck. "Here was a man fifty-six years old, world-famous and much admired," Hedin wrote in his memoirs, "and here I was, a young and ambitious student who had done nothing remarkable except a reckless ride across Persia" (1950, 1:136). But Richthofen received him in a truly friendly way and suggested that Sven attend his lectures and enroll in his seminar.

In 1889 Europe dominated the world, and Berlin, along with London, Paris, Vienna, and Saint Petersburg, was one of its great capitals. Germany's trade and industry were already a serious rival of England's, which led the world; and Germany's military might had begun to rival that of Russia, the largest military power in Europe. German universities, too, were considered among the world's best; their influence was strong even across the Atlantic, where American post-graduate education closely followed the German model. Hedin came from a small country and found himself in a world capital. Germany molded his views, his lifestyle, his values. For the rest of his life, he thought of Germany as the center of the world and the paragon of all virtues, and he looked upon Germans as a chosen people who could do no wrong.

Besides taking courses under the two leading geographers at the University of Berlin, Richthofen and Kiepert, Hedin took part in Richthofen's weekly seminars. These were always held in the evening. One or two students spoke on a subject they had studied in great detail, there was a discussion led by the professor, and afterward all, including Richthofen, adjourned to a nearby tavern for sandwiches and beer. The word for these informal gatherings was *Nachspiel,* the German equivalent of postlude, and for the rest of his life Hedin used that word to refer to the informal talks over beer or wine or brandy that followed important meetings. Richthofen usually stayed only for a short while, and after his departure serious beer drinking began and usually lasted until the small hours of the morning. But it was the seminar itself and the exchange of views during and immediately after it that impressed Hedin. Richthofen remained his ideal and Germany the country he admired most.

His fellow students in Richthofen's seminar impressed him, and his judgment was borne out in later years, when they in turn became world figures in geography: von Drygalski was one of the great authorities on the polar world; Schott was one of the founders of modern oceanography; Kretschmer became a world leader in studies on the history of geography and mapmaking; Phillipson's life work on the Mediterranean lands still stands as a model of careful and inspired regional geography.

Hedin's first seminar presentation was on the explorations of the Russian, Przhevalsky, in Chinese Central Asia. He drew a large map of Central Asia to illustrate his paper, and Richthofen followed its preparation with great interest, recognizing the young

Swede's skill in mapmaking. When it was almost finished, the professor looked it over carefully, then pointed his finger to the eastern Himalayas, where the great rivers of China and Southeast Asia have their sources: the Yangtze, the Mekong, the Salween, the Irawaddy. "You will be the one who will explore this unknown area some day," said Richthofen, setting a goal for Hedin's further work. As things turned out, Hedin never visited the area, but Richthofen's words were the equivalent of a blessing, an expression of confidence in Hedin's ability to make a contribution to the geography of Asia.

On February 4, 1890, Hedin had his day in the Berlin seminar on geography. Not only did all the students turn out for the occasion, but so did the Swedish minister to Berlin, as an invited guest of the speaker. All went very well. Richthofen liked Hedin's paper but was especially impressed with his map, and when Hedin offered to present it to the Institute of Geography, the professor was visibly pleased. The next day, Hedin was a dinner guest at the Swedish minister's house and very much the man of the hour.

Richthofen was a man of formal manners, in the tradition of German universities, but obviously he also enjoyed getting together with his favorite students in an informal fashion, and Hedin was definitely one of the chosen few. He was a guest at his professor's house for a number of dinners, admired his host's great library, and met not only important scholars but members of the German aristocracies of birth, money, and talent as well. The five months he spent in Berlin, from late October, 1889, until April, 1890, were the most exciting and inspiring he had ever experienced. The memory of those days stayed with him always.

Five months' study does not sound very impressive in retrospect, yet Hedin obviously learned a great deal during that time. Richthofen, a good judge of men, recognized his student's lack of detailed knowledge; he was anxious to have him follow a regular course of studies and in due time go forth to solve the mysteries of the structure of the Eastern Himalayas and their relationship to the mountain systems of China and Southeast Asia. But Hedin was not patient enough to stay at the university. Many years later, writing his memoirs, he admitted as much.

I was just not up to his expectations. I had already been out in the wilds of Asia, perhaps too early on. I had enjoyed too much the splendour and beauty of the Orient, the silence and loneliness of the desert, and could not accept the idea of spending any more time in a seat in the lecture hall. My lack of training in geology that Richthofen wanted to fill in was to be with me through decades of explorations in Asia. I found myself at a parting of the ways in Berlin: it was a matter of spending the years of my youth acquiring a solid academic foundation in geology, or follow my vocation and as a pioneer open those parts of Central Asia that were either unknown, or only little known, so that systematic research could be carried out by specialists. I chose the second alternative. (1950, 138–39)

IV

To Persia and the Gates of China, 1890–91

In April, 1890, Hedin returned to Stockholm to have his diplomat's uniform fitted and to prepare for his second journey to
Persia. This time he was a member of an official mission, but
secretly he hoped to do some traveling on his own as well.

The mission was headed by Treschow, an official of the court
of Sweden. Count Lewenhaupt was the mission's military attaché,
and von Geijer, a career diplomat stationed at the Swedish legation in Turkey, was its secretary. Hedin's function was that of an
interpreter, both in Turkish and in Persian.

The mission left Stockholm for Berlin, Vienna, and points east.
Richthofen, anxious that his student should take advantage of his
travels, introduced him to colleagues in Vienna, and during the
mission's brief stay there Hedin met two of the outstanding earth
scientists of the time, Albrecht Penck and Eduard Suess, both professors at the University of Vienna. He also had the opportunity to
meet the Austrian geologist Tietze, who had carried out important
studies in northern Persia; he gave the young Swede tips on where
to go and what to see in the region surrounding Tehran.

The mission's next stop was Constantinople, where they were
received by the sultan of Turkey, who gave Hedin the Order of
Medjidie. It was his first such honor from a foreign potentate;
many others followed, and Hedin never tired of showing them to
his visitors.

The trip continued by steamer across the Black Sea, then by
train across the Russian territory of the Trans-Caucasus. The only
real excitement of the entire journey occurred during that train
trip from the port of Batumi on the Black Sea to Baku on the
Caspian. There was no dining car, but the train stopped long
enough at some stations to allow travelers to get a hasty meal in

the station restaurant. During the stops, the train conductor looked after the diplomats' luggage, but they carried with them the small leather bag containing the decoration that was to be presented to the shah of Persia. While at lunch one day, the head of the mission put the bag down by his seat, and when the bell announcing the departure of the train sounded, the diplomats returned to their carriage. Only then did they discover that the bag containing the decoration was missing. Hedin, the youngest of the group, was dispatched to find it. The delegation was in luck: the bag was where they had left it. Speculating what would have happened if someone had taken it, one of the diplomats said that the only thing they could have done would have been to commit suicide. Not so, said Hedin, a practical soul, we would have telegraphed home and asked for a replacement!

The mission's brief stay in Tehran was filled with pomp and ceremony. But when time came for their return to Sweden, Hedin had other ideas. Technically, he was a member of the Swedish foreign service while serving with the mission to Persia, and he would need permission if he wanted to leave it before completing the voyage home. Instead of asking the minister of foreign affairs for leave, Hedin telegraphed to King Oscar II, requesting leave to undertake a journey to Russian Central Asia and to Kashgar, the westernmost city in China.

King Oscar II had a lifelong interest in voyages of exploration. Some time earlier, in the years 1878 through 1880, he had been one of the contributors to the expenses of Nordenskiöld's great expedition to the Northeast Passage. Here was one of his young subjects already acquainted with parts of Asia and anxious to know more. The king granted Hedin's request.

After the other members of the expedition left Persia, Hedin stayed behind in Tehran, once more a guest of Dr. Hybennet. By now it was the beginning of July and time for the shah's yearly vacation, a trip to Mount Damavand, the peak that dominates the mountains north of Tehran, to escape for a few days the summer heat of the capital. Dr. Hybennet, ever the thoughtful host, asked the shah for permission for his young countryman to take part in the great trek, and Hedin joined the imperial caravan.

The trip was an outing on a gigantic scale, for the entire court followed the shah to Mount Damavand, bedding down every night in a camp made up of hundreds of tents. To Hedin, the journey had another purpose. Accompanied by two native guides and carrying his own instruments—barometer and thermometer—to make observations during the climb, he went all the way to the peak. Getting to a place that is over five thousand meters high was something of a mountaineering feat, though it had been done before, and Hedin's measurement of the height of Mount Damavand turned out to be inaccurate. But he took copious notes, observed the weather, vegetation, and snow and ice conditions, and two years later assembled the information into a publication of his own.

Back in Tehran, Hedin packed his gear for the trip eastward. He was better equipped than on his first journey four years earlier, and though he did not have much money, he hoped to complete his journey across eastern Persia into Russian Central Asia, and crossing the Pamir Highlands, to enter into China.

The complex structure of mountain systems, high plateaus, and basins that is Central Asia was known in its general outlines by the last decade of the nineteenth century. The core of the entire structure is a set of high mountains and plateaus known as the Pamirs, called by the people of the region the "top of the world." From the Pamirs, great mountains extend in several directions. To the west, these mountains, forming a pattern of arcs, surround the interior plateaus of Afghanistan and Iran. To the north and northeast, the Alai and other lesser ranges form the southern boundaries of Russian territory.

East of the Pamirs, the Tien Shan (the "Heavenly Mountains," as they are known to the Chinese) separate two basins, Dzungaria to the north and the Tarim Basin to the south. Further to the south, the Kunlun Mountains form the southern limits of the Tarim Basin and the northern boundary of Tibet, then as now a Chinese-controlled land.

Southeast from the Pamirs the Karakoram range sweeps across Tibet. Further southeast still, the world's highest mountain system, the Himalayas, form the boundary between Tibet and India.

Of these mighty mountains, the Himalayas were then best known, as a result of the pioneer surveys carried out by the British from their base in India throughout the nineteenth century. Individual Russian, British, and French explorers had contributed to the knowledge of the vast complex of mountains and basins north of the Himalayas, but there remained enough unknown territory to justify further careful, detailed exploration. The exact height of many mountain peaks was still to be determined, the sources of the great rivers that traverse the area, the Brahmaputra and the Indus, were yet to be identified, and the outline and nature of the region's inland lakes were not yet fully known. For the next two decades, Sven Hedin crisscrossed Central Asia on his expeditions, and much of our present knowledge of Tibet and of the Tarim Basin is based on his discoveries.

On September 9, 1890, Hedin left Tehran, traveling east across northern Persia. Moving along the old and well-trodden routes of the caravans, he filled his notebooks with observations and sketched people, buildings, and animals wherever he went. Only once did he leave the caravan route, to take a close look at the great salt desert of northern Persia, the Dasht-i-Kavir. Fifteen years later, he returned there as a seasoned explorer to investigate and map what was truly unknown territory.

The most interesting part of his journey across northeast Persia was his visit to Mashhad, a city almost as sacred as Mecca itself to Persians, who are members of the Shiite sect of Islam. To be buried in Mashhad was the ambition of all Persians who could afford to have their coffins carried there, and many a caravan bound for Mashhad consisted of a cargo of coffins.

All his life Hedin was fascinated with camels. Some of his best drawings are portraits of those great beasts of burden. In one of his letters home, written in 1890, he described meeting a caravan at night.

Of a sudden one hears the muted sound of bells far away. It is a strange music, it creates an impression that is magical and it makes one sleepy. The sound gets more and more precise, finally it is very close. Like huge black ghosts, the camels appear out of the darkness; slowly, majestically, with dignity they move across the desert sands. (October, 1890)

From Mashhad, Hedin turned north, and crossing the mountains that separate Iran from the wide expanses of what at the time was called Turkestan, he entered Russian territory. The Russians had conquered the vast area lying between the Caspian Sea and the high mountain ranges of the Pamirs, in long military campaigns during the 1860s and 1870s. To consolidate their rule, they built a railroad from the port of Krasnovodsk on the east shore of the Caspian to their capital, Tashkent. Hedin traveled on that rail line and was cordially received by the Russian authorities. He was provided with letters of introduction to commanders of Russian army posts near the Russian-Chinese border. What seems even more surprising, given the Russian tradition of secrecy, the governor-general of Central Asia gave orders that the young Swede be provided with the latest maps of the Pamirs, the Russian-Chinese frontier zone.

By the time Hedin reached the last sizable Russian outpost, the town of Osh, it was late November. Ahead of him lay the vast mountain mass of the Pamirs, which was difficult to cross under the best of conditions. Its only roads were narrow trails used by caravans and by couriers carrying mail to Russian consulates in westernmost China.

The Russian commander at Osh tried his best to persuade Hedin that it was too late in the season to attempt a crossing of the Pamirs. But when Hedin insisted on going ahead, his Russian host saw to it that he had enough warm clothing, helped him hire the best of local guides and good horses, and even sent a man ahead to lay in a cache of food and a tent near the high pass Hedin planned to cross.

It was a rough journey early in December, when dangerous storms could sweep across the Pamirs, and in places the horses barely made it across deep snow and along treacherous trails. But when Hedin reached the highest point on his trip, the Terek Davan Pass, the view made all difficulties seem light. From just below the pass he could see the vast mountain masses, resplendent in snow and ice, stretch far into the distance, pointing the way to the Tarim Basin and even toward Tibet. These were lands Hedin hoped to explore some day.

A short distance further he came upon the Russian-Chinese frontier, and beyond it, the Chinese border post. Hedin did not have a visa to enter China, but instead of being turned back, he was most cordially received by the Chinese official in charge, who, delighted to have a traveler pass by his remote outpost so late in the season, conveniently forgot to ask for Hedin's travel documents. He could thus continue on his way, and as the trail became a road of sorts, he gradually left the high mountains behind. On December 14, he entered Kashgar, the westernmost town in China.

Kashgar is the most important of the oases situated along the rim of the Tarim Basin, an area consisting almost entirely of desert. Most of the oasis-dwellers are not Chinese but are instead closely related to the populations living across the mountain barrier under Russian rule. Like them, they speak a language related to Turkish; and they tap the water courses on the mountainous rim of the basin to irrigate their fields of grain, vegetables, and fruit. Hedin found their intricate irrigation systems fascinating.

Kashgar itself had at one time been an important stop on the caravan routes of Central Asia, but by the late 1800s it was merely a remote backwater of China, considered a place of exile by Chinese officials assigned there. Hedin, once more enjoying the hospitality of a fellow European, the Russian consul general, did not really want to spend much time in Kashgar; he had hoped to continue eastward, all the way to Peking. But the Chinese governor turned down his request for permission to travel further in Chinese territory and asked him to return to Russia by the shortest possible route.

One more Hedin was in luck. Three Russian cavalrymen posted as guards at the Russian consulate in Kashgar were about to leave for home at the end of their tour of duty, and Hedin was able to join them. When he left Kashgar, it was Christmas Eve for him, but not for his Russian companions, who still followed the Old Style calendar; for them the date was December 13.

The small group of riders crossed the great Tien Shan range

north of Kashgar and arrived at the first Russian military post, Narin, on December 31. Hedin could have continued with his Russian companions, but he was not quite ready to do so. A few days' ride away, on the shores of Lake Issyk Kul, high in the mountains, was the grave of the great Russian explorer Przhevalsky, whose work Hedin had translated only two years earlier. He visited the spot, then turned north toward the lowlands of Russian Turkestan, to the railroad, to begin the long journey home.

Sven Hedin returned to Stockholm on March 29, 1891, after almost a year's traveling. The journey, like the ride across Persia, was more a matter of getting better acquainted with Asia than a scientific expedition. Even his sister Alma, writing about it, had to admit that "from a scientific point of view the trip was not of particularly great importance" (A. Hedin 1925, 36–37).

What Hedin learned on this, his second trip to Asia, was the need for good equipment, for servants, guides, saddle horses, and pack animals. He had been able to make two trips on very limited funds, but he knew that to make his mark he needed more time and a lot more money. He also knew that before he could start rounding up financial support he would need proper university credentials, an advanced degree from a good university, preferably in Germany. And that was the next major step he undertook: he returned to Germany to complete his doctorate.

V

Preparing for the First Expedition

In the fall of 1891, less than six months after Hedin returned to Sweden, his book describing his latest journey, *King Oscar's Embassy to the Shah of Persia in 1890*, was published in Stockholm. It was a volume of nearly five hundred pages, and it bore witness to Hedin's skill in using his letters home and his travel diaries to produce sizable books in unbelievably short time. He wrote in longhand and had a member of his family make a clean copy. As the archivist who was in charge of arranging Hedin's papers when they were deposited in the Swedish National Archives put it, "Hedin had a family office force at his disposal" (Holm 1974, 17).

A few months after the appearance of *King Oscar's Embassy*, another work, *Across Khorasan and Turkestan*, in two volumes totaling more than five hundred pages, appeared, again in Stockholm. It was a description of Hedin's journey from Tehran across Persia and Russian Central Asia to Kashgar and back, and together with the previously published book it served as the foundation for Hedin's subsequent career as an immensely popular travel writer.

The two books were out, copies were duly sent to Richthofen's geographical institute and to the Geographical Society in Berlin, and Hedin turned to his main concern, that of getting proper academic credentials. What he needed was a doctorate in geography from a recognized university. There was still no department of geography in any Swedish university, and besides, Hedin knew that Richthofen considered him one of his favorites. In April, 1892, he returned to Berlin to ask Richthofen's help and counsel.

Richthofen liked Sven Hedin. He found him a man of immense energy and ambition and a born explorer, but too impatient to spend more time to acquire an advanced degree than was absolutely necessary and certainly not interested in immersing himself in academic studies. Two years earlier, Hedin had told Richthofen that instead of returning to the University of Berlin, he was going off on a journey to Persia. The great geographer recognized the impatience of his student to get out in the field, to see faraway places and follow new trails. Richthofen wrote Hedin in the fall of 1890:

> I am sorry that the great things you are doing now have taken precedence over studies in the Alps with Professors Heim and Teller. When it comes to mountains, though you have done some good basic work, you will have to proceed as a self-taught man. Your excellent powers of observation will help, for in this business common sense helps most. (1933, 74–75)

Hedin had hoped to complete his doctorate under Richthofen, but he was advised by his master, as Hedin referred to him throughout his life, to seek his degree elsewhere. "He suggested," Hedin wrote home on May 6, 1892, "that I pursue studies of the way geography is taught at another university, and spend a few weeks in Halle, with Professor Kirchoff" (1933, 36).

Although Richthofen did not believe that Hedin could complete his degree at his own institute, he liked the young Swede far too much not to help him in other ways. To establish Hedin before the German geographers as an explorer, Richthofen, president of the prestigious Berlin Geographical Society, invited him to speak to the group about his recent journey. On June 11, 1892, Hedin presented a lecture entitled "Mount Demavend as Seen Through My Own Observations" (1892, 304–22).

The evening was a success. Hedin was introduced by Richthofen, who mentioned the fact that Hedin had already published three books on his travels and had presented them to the society's library. After the lecture, it was Richthofen again who thanked the speaker, spoke of his iron will and energy, mentioned his plans for future travels, and expressed the hope that after his next journey to Tibet he would again speak to the society. Last but not least, the second speaker of the evening, reporting on recent explorations in Tibet, used the large map of Central Asia that Hedin had drawn three years earlier and presented to Richthofen's institute.

After the lecture there was a dinner; Hedin sat in the place of honor, on Richthofen's right. In his letter home, he reported on the people who sat next or opposite him, on what was served at the dinner, and what the conversation at the table was about. That sort of detailed reporting became a habit, and for the rest of his long life, in his letters and in his diaries, he always included such information.

Two days after his lecture at the Berlin Geographical Society, Hedin went to Halle and was given a warm welcome by the head of the geographical institute, Professor Kirchhoff. He spent the next six weeks there, except for a trip to Berlin to address Richthofen's seminar, and studied hard for examinations in philosophy, geology, and geography.

The dissertation Hedin submitted for his doctorate was the paper he had earlier presented to the Berlin Geographical Society—that is, his description of his ascent of the volcano, Mount Damavand, in Persia. Then and later he always managed to get the maximum use out of everything he wrote. On July 28, 1892, he passed his examinations and advised his family of the results in a telegram of unusual brevity: "Dr. Phil." (doctor of philosophy). He got what he wanted, a doctor's degree from a German university, and his academic career ended there. The dissertation was published in the proceedings of the Berlin Geographical Society, since it had first been presented as a lecture there.

"Mount Demavend as Seen Through My Own Observations" is a brief statement, thirty-one pages long. Better than half of it is a written survey of what people who had climbed the mountain before Hedin had written about it. This is followed by a short account of Hedin's own climb, some observations on geological features of the mountain, and a description of how his readings of temperatures and barometric pressures were converted into the figure he gives for the height of Mount Damavand, 5,465 meters. The actual figure is 5,771 meters, and thus Hedin's error is 5.3 percent, a permissible one given the fact that his instruments were not fully reliable.

Back home, Hedin set to work to prepare for his next journey. This time, it would no longer be a matter of merely getting acquainted with Central Asia. Now that he had acquired proper credentials, he was going to bring back important scientific results, not just material for travel books. The problem, as for all explorers at all times, was that of funds.

King Oscar II looked favorably upon Swedes who by means of scientific expeditions would shed glory on their country. When Hedin approached him for help, the king promised a substantial sum. An old friend of the Hedin family collected another goodly amount from friends of geography in the big industrial and commercial city of Göteborg, while Hedin called upon people of means to ask for assistance. Among these was J. V. Smitt, one of the wealthiest men in Sweden. Smitt listened to Hedin's plans attentively and offered the young explorer an excellent cigar. Hedin departed in high spirits, convinced that a big contribution was on its way, but found out afterwards that offering a cigar was Smitt's way of turning people down. The visit was not a total failure, however, for Smitt gave Hedin a fine hunting rifle to take on his trip.

By September, 1892, a respectable sum, 30,000 kronor, at the time the equivalent of 8,400 dollars, had accumulated in Hedin's travel fund. Then help of another kind came his way. He was invited to speak to the Imperial Russian Geographical Society in Saint Petersburg. His Swedish friends there, including Carl and Emanuel Nobel, prominent industrialists who had oil fields in the Caucasus and chemical plants in Russia and elsewhere, were worried when Hedin told them that he planned to address the group in Russian. Their fears were unfounded. The lecture went so well, and the Russian audience, composed of distinguished scholars and high-ranking military men, was so delighted with it, that the chief of the Geographical Section of the Russian General Staff, General Stebnitzky, told Hedin afterward that the society would honor him with its silver medal.

Seldom did Hedin's public lectures have such a lasting effect on his fortunes as the one he gave in Saint Petersburg in 1892. He became an overnight sensation and met everyone of importance not only among Russian geographers but among government officials and army officers who had an interest in Central Asia. This was a time when the two empires, Britain and Russia, were in direct competition for control of the heart of Asia, even though they never engaged in open conflict. It is possible to speculate that Sven Hedin, citizen of a neutral country, acute observer, successful writer, appealed to the Russians as an ideal emissary who, without any hidden motives, could provide valuable information on Central Asia.

Hedin met the chief of the Russian General Staff and was promised free transport for himself and his equipment anywhere in the Russian Empire. He was received by the Chinese ambassador to Russia and given letters of introduction and a special passport for travel in Chinese Central Asia. After a long conversation with Hedin, the dean of Russian geographers, Veniamin Semenov, gave him a warm letter of introduction to the governor of the province of Orenburg, on the borders of Asiatic Russia.

Dr. Hedin, a Swedish explorer and member of our Imperial Geographical Society is bound for Tashkent and beyond. Please give him all assistance so he can get proper attention at the post stations on his way. . . . In a word, whatever you can do for him shall be considered as if done for me and our Society. I am too old now to travel, so I enjoy helping young explorers. (December 12, 1892)

Last but not least, the Nobel brothers promised that if the funds Hedin was collecting in Sweden were not sufficient for his journey, they would help. They were as good as their word, and at the last moment, before Hedin's departure, they did give him a substantial sum for his travel costs.

The winter of 1892–93 was over, funds were coming in, albeit slowly, and Hedin was in good spirits; then he got another eye infection, and this time it spread to his good eye. He suffered much pain, had to have an operation, and for over three months, from mid-April until early August, was very ill. The eye specialist did all he could but told the family that he did not believe Hedin would recover sufficiently ever to be able to travel, much less to explore. But Hedin's iron will and the expert medical care he received resulted in a minor miracle: by late September, he had completely recovered and was ready to take off for Asia.

One looks in vain in Hedin's voluminous writings for any mention of his constant worry about his eye. He knew that the inflammation could occur at any time, and in fact he did have a recurrence in 1894, in the wilds of the Pamir Highlands. It was the only health problem he had. He overcame it, and did more than that; with only one good eye, he managed to draw thousands of maps, sketches, and panoramas of reasonable accuracy even for someone with perfect sight.

By mid-October, 1893, Hedin was ready to start on what he considered his first scientific expedition, to Chinese Central Asia, Tibet, and Mongolia. Earlier that year, when he had asked King Oscar II for help, he had stated his principal objectives in a brief memorandum. These included making a large-scale map of his entire route; determining geographical coordinates (longitude, latitude, and altitude) wherever possible; making geological investigations and collections of rock samples; studying the peoples of Central Asia, including their customs, their appearance, their languages, and even making anthropometric measurements; undertaking archaeological researches for ruined cities; making photographs of places of interest; making meteorological observations; undertaking hydrographic investigations, including measuring the depths of lakes and water volume in streams; collecting plants; and "keeping of a diary during the entire journey" (1898, 1:v–ix, 18–22).

Part of Hedin's original plan for this expedition was to employ a Swedish assistant whose duty it would be to take astronomical observations. That idea was dropped. Hedin went alone, partly, as he put it, "for the sake of economy," and partly "because I did not like the idea of being involved in dangers and hardships which I could endure myself, but in which a companion might not have cared to risk his life" (1898, 1:23–24). On this and on his two subsequent expeditions, Hedin employed only Asiatics as guides, camel drivers, and servants. As to scientific peers, he preferred to go it alone.

October is a cool month in Stockholm, and nights are likely to be cold; by the time Hedin started on his way across Russia, he would encounter winter. Others might have preferred to wait until spring, a better season for traveling across frozen lands, but Hedin was not a patient man when it came to exploring. He was ready to go. On October 16, 1893, he set out for Asia for the third time.

VI

The First Expedition, 1894–97

It was early November when Hedin arrived in Orenburg, the end of the railroad line that connected Saint Petersburg with the eastern part of European Russia. He had already traveled some 2,200 kilometers, but 2,000 more lay ahead before he would reach his first goal, Tashkent, the capital of Russian Central Asia. And the only means of travel was by carriage.

He had equipped himself for the cold with heavy felt boots, a sheepskin coat, blankets for the bottom of the carriage to ease the jolting ride, and blankets for protection from the bitter cold. Traveling through the open, snow-covered grasslands was monotonous. In a letter he wrote:

> The steppe looks like a huge frozen lake; the heavy carriage rolls at a good pace. Yet were it not for the telegraph poles, one would believe the carriage stood still, looking at the horizon. One does not meet anyone walking, anyone riding, any caravan, only a few native Kirghiz, and those only once in a great while. (November 20, 1893)

It took him nineteen days to cover the distance to Tashkent, changing horses at post stations, stopping for tea and some food, taking photographs, sketching. At long last, on December 4, he arrived in Tashkent, where temperatures were well above freezing and where Russian hospitality awaited him.

Hedin stayed there nearly two months, getting his instruments—barometer, thermometer, hygrometer, clocks—in shape, laying in provisions for himself and his servants for the next stage of his journey, and buying trinkets to be presented to the natives

39

and Chinese officials he knew he would encounter. Finally, on January 25, 1894, he set out to cross the Pamirs.

Once again, he chose a difficult time of the year to travel. The Pamirs are high mountain country, passes of over 4,000 meters had to be crossed, snowstorms were frequent, and most of the Russian officials considered it foolish to undertake the journey in midwinter. But Hedin was not about to wait; he wanted to get across the Pamirs and to the border of Chinese Central Asia. He hired horses to carry his supplies and natives to accompany him as guides and drivers. He was in luck. He crossed the mountains without running into severe storms, avalanches, or landslides, and by mid-March he made it all the way to the most distant outpost of the Russian Empire, Fort Pamir, or Pamirsky Post.

The Pamirs were at that time the place where three empires met. Russia controlled the western and northern approaches, China held the eastern gates, and British India ruled over the southern outliers. The boundaries separating these nations were far from being well marked, and it was only during this decade, the 1890s, that a series of agreements, followed by the actual demarcation of the boundary, laid to rest the possibility of armed conflict in these remote highlands. Hedin was welcomed by the officers of Fort Pamir as a fellow European and was entertained royally; he was also given advice on his plans to explore the Pamirs, and he and his caravan had a chance to rest.

The next goal was one of the high peaks of the Pamirs, Muztagh-Ata (Father of Icy Mountains), 7,546 meters above sea level. It was during his first attempt to climb that peak that Hedin realized the qualities of his Uzbek guide, Islam Bai. Islam Bai was the only one of his native companions of whom Hedin ever spoke in his books, and he paid him the highest tribute.

When he first came to see me I was a perfect stranger to him, and he had no conception of the real object of my journey. Nevertheless he willingly left his peaceful home at Osh [in Russian Central Asia] to share with me all the dangers and perils of a protracted journey through the heart of Asia. We traveled side by side through the terrible desert, facing its sandstorms in company, and nearly perishing of thirst; and when my other attendants fell by the side of the track, overcome by the hardships of the journey, Islam Bai, with unselfish devotion, stuck by my maps and drawings, and was thus instrumental in saving what I so highly prized. When we scaled the snowy precipices, he was always in the van, leading the way. He guided the caravan with a sure hand through the foaming torrents of the Pamirs. He kept faithful and vigilant watch when the Tanguts threatened to molest us. In a word, the services this man rendered were incalculable. But for him I can truthfully say that my journey would not have had such a fortunate termination as it had. (1898, 1:100–101)

As it turned out, Hedin's first attempt to climb Muztagh-Ata failed, because a new attack of iritis forced him to leave the mountains and seek rest and relief in Kashgar, at the house of his friend from the preceding journey, the Russian consul-general Petrovsky. In Kashgar, he made friends with the Chinese governor and was thus able to move through Chinese territory without trouble from local officials.

By late June, he felt well enough to make another attempt to conquer Muztagh-Ata, which had become something of a personal challenge. It was a good time for the journey, and he was well equipped. He had Tibetan yaks (sturdy pack animals that are used to high altitudes) and servants who stuck to his side. On his second and third attempts, he reached higher and higher levels on the mountain, but he could not make it to the peak. Hedin, who was not a skilled mountain climber, was trying to climb one of the highest peaks in the whole of the Pamir Highlands. He failed, but he brought back a mass of valuable observations on the high mountain lakes, streams, and glaciers and mapped the Muztagh-Ata massif for the first time.

In a passage in his book on the expedition, Hedin summed up his fascination with high places. Stepping outside his tiny tent on a night of full moon and clear skies, he saw a magnificent panorama.

The rocky wall immediately in front of me lay in such deep shadow that I could barely distinguish where its transparent ice-mantle ended and the black mountain-wall began. To the left and a few hundred yards above me, the outermost parts of the glacier were bathed in the moonlight. . . . Light clouds, dancing before the gentle southern breeze, formed in rapid succession concentric rings, halos, and the like in all the colors of the rainbow. . . . A dead silence everywhere—not an echo from the opposite wall of rock. . . . The breathing of the yaks was visible, but not audible. The animals stood silent and motionless. . . . The clouds flitted noiseless by. . . . A curious feeling of being at a vast distance from the earth took possession of me. It was difficult to realize that the four continents lay actually below my feet; and that a girdle drawn around the earth at the level where I stood would cut off only the tops of a very few mountains in Asia and South America. . . . I seemed to be standing on the confines of space—cold, silent, boundless. (1898, 1:372–73)

Summer came to an end in the Pamir Highlands, and Hedin and his small caravan returned to the safe haven of Kashgar and the hospitable home of the Russian consul-general, where he spent the worst of the winter of 1894–95. He caught up on his voluminous correspondence, wrote several reports on the results of his travels in the Pamirs and sent them to Richthofen in Berlin, and felt ready by early January, 1895, to start out on a new venture. He wanted to travel into the deserts of Chinese Central Asia.

Kashgar, the town where Hedin returned time after time from the rigors of exploration, is one of the oases in the Tarim Basin, the southern half of China's westernmost region, Sinkiang. The basin is a large area, nearly 1,200 kilometers from west to east and nearly 600 kilometers wide from north to south. It is enclosed by the Pamirs in the west, the Tien Shan, or Heavenly Mountains, in the north, and the Kunlun and Altyn Tagh Mountains in the south, but it is open to the east, toward the rest of China. Virtually all of the Tarim Basin is desert, but the streams descending into it from the surrounding mountains create a series of oases along its northern and southern rim. Its principal stream is the Tarim River, which is created by the confluence of several lesser streams at its western end; other rivers, with their sources along the southern rim, remain dry watercourses most of the year and fill up only after there is heavy snowfall in the mountains. The core of the basin is known as the Takla Makan Desert, the westernmost part of the desert belt that extends from Mongolia to the foothills of the Pamirs.

Hedin was not the first to fall under the spell of the desert. During the thirteenth century, Marco Polo, greatest of all medieval travelers, crossed the area on his way from Europe to China; he called it the Desert of Lop, after the town he said was located in its northeastern section.

Little had changed during the six centuries that separated the travels of Polo and Hedin. Marco Polo describes with remarkable accuracy the people of the desert, the way travelers prepared to cross it by resting beforehand, and the fact that the caravans used camels in preference to other beasts of burden because "they carry heavy burdens and are fed with a small quantity of provender." He reported that the desert was believed to be haunted by evil spirits who led travelers lagging behind their caravan astray and left them to die.

> Marvelous indeed and almost passing belief are the stories related of these spirits of the desert, which are said at times to fill the air with the sounds of all kinds of musical instruments, and also of drums and the clash of arms.

Before making camp for the night, said Marco Polo, travelers set up a sign pointing the direction they would want to follow the next day and attached bells to their animals to keep them from straggling (*From the Travels of Marco Polo the Venetian* [New York, 1918], 99–101).

Richthofen, in a letter he sent to Hedin during the winter of 1893–94, warned him that in "selecting your route you should not be unduly influenced by the desire to choose only those routes where no one else had traveled. As a rule, there is a great deal left to be done in areas not traversed by careful observers" (1933, 95–96). But Hedin kept hearing about lost cities in the area of the Tarim Basin that the local people called the Mankiller Desert. "I had fallen under the spell of the weird witchcraft of the desert," he wrote. "I knew that beyond the sand dunes, amid the grave-like silence, stretched the unknown, enchanted land, of whose existence not even the oldest records make mention, the land that I was going to be the first to tread" (1898, 1:449).

On February 17, 1895, Hedin, accompanied by his servant Islam Bai, set out from Kashgar bound for the worst part of the Takla Makan Desert. It took weeks to round up good camels to make the journey and to hire men who knew the desert and would be reliable guides. At long last, Islam Bai returned to the small town of Merket on the western edge of the desert where Hedin had been waiting with eight strong camels and three men. They were all local people who had gone into the desert before to look for gold, and one of them claimed that he knew all the trails and would lead the small caravan across the desert wastes with ease. His name was Kasim, as was that of another of the newly hired men, and to distinguish between them they called him by his nickname, Yollchi (the scout).

Hedin's plan for crossing the Takla Makan was to start from its western margin and travel until he found a low mountain called Mazar Tagh, which was very near a stream called the Khotan Darya, one of several that crossed the desert from its southern, mountainous fringe to the Tarim River in the north. Hedin estimated that the crossing could be accomplished in a fortnight if he averaged eighteen kilometers a day. This was a reasonable estimate for a caravan composed of determined men riding strong camels.

It was while getting ready for this journey that Hedin first tried out his own method for mapping his route, one that is appealing in its simplicity and thoroughly reliable in its results. He measured a base line of 400 meters and timed the interval between start and finish, riding his camel. Later, seated on the camel, he used a compass and a watch, noted distance and direction in his sketchbook, and every evening, using his notes, drew a map of the day's journey. By the end of his 1894–97 expedition, he had drawn 552 such maps. On each one he noted the terrain, whether it was clayey, sandy, or stony; wrote his observations on the vegetation; and marked important features of the landscape.

On April 10, Hedin and his four servants started on their journey amidst the cries of the local people, who were afraid that the group would not return from the desert alive. Within three days, they came across the first completely barren area but found a spring and were able to replenish their water casks. On the sixth day they were still riding faster than they had planned, covering twenty-eight kilometers that day. "We were getting farther and farther into the unknown ocean of sandy desert," Hedin wrote later. "Not a sign of life to be seen, not a sound to be heard, except the monotonous ding-dong of the bells tinkling in time to the soft tramping of the camels" (1898, 1:497).

On the tenth day they came to an area of "moist, luxuriant grass, thickly studded with glittering pools and marshes" (1898, 1:503). Hedin was so impressed with the change that he called the stretch "an earthly paradise." There was water available, and he ordered that the casks should be half-filled, to reduce the burden of the camels; he was convinced that that much water would last at least ten days. His native scout, Yollchi, assured him that they were not more than four days away from the Khotan River.

On the thirteenth day, they encountered really imposing sand dunes for the first time, some as many as fifteen to seventeen meters high, and the pace of the caravan slowed down. On the fourteenth day a sandstorm came up.

> Clouds and columns of sand whirled in a mad dance across the desert, so that every now and again we became entirely swallowed up in them. . . . The horizon was veiled in an unbroken yellowish-red haze. The fine red drift-sand penetrated everywhere—into mouth, nose, ears; even our clothes became impregnated with it. . . . (1898, 1:516)

But the storm passed, and though by now they should have reached the river, Hedin was not alarmed. The next day, however, he discovered that the casks had not been properly filled and that the four men, eight camels, and two dogs along with the six sheep, half-dozen hens, and cock they had taken along for provisions had only enough enough water to last two more days. Two of the camels had to be abandoned that day, their loads transferred to the surviving beasts. When the men tried to dig a well, it turned out to be dry.

On April 27, seventeen days after they set out, there was no sign of the line on the horizon that would signal the trees that were supposed to mark the Khotan River. One of the men insisted that they had come under a spell of witchcraft and would never find their way out of the desert. The next day, after weathering another sandstorm, Hedin decided to leave behind much of their remaining food as well as his books; he marked the site in the hope of returning there. Two days later, on April 30, there was no water left in the casks. Hedin's last entry into his diary on that day read, "We are all terribly weak, men as well as camels. God help us all!" (1898, 1:552).

On the first of May, after three weeks in the desert, Hedin and his men had little hope that they would survive. They tried to drink some strong Chinese brandy that they carried for use in their spirit stove, but all got sick. The oldest of the men died, and so did two more camels. Two days later, Hedin's faithful servant, Islam Bai, could no longer walk, and the local scout, Yollchi, had disappeared. Hedin and Kasim, one of the natives, staggered on for another day, until on May 5, Hedin saw the line of trees that signified water and life and found a pool of sweet water. After drinking until he felt that his strength had returned, he filled his boots with water, retraced his steps, and found his servant Kasim, who had lain down to die.

Together, Hedin and Kasim set out to find help and food, and the next day, May 6, they ran into a small group of shepherds who gave them food and shelter. Four days later Islam Bai caught up with Hedin, who was resting on the banks of the Khotan River. He had been found by travelers and had revived and returned to his master. He was leading the only surviving camel, which carried two of Hedin's rifles, some of his instruments, and his diary and maps.

A few days later, Hedin and Islam Bai returned to the place where they had left their supplies and the rest of the instruments, but they were gone. Hedin's precious barometer was missing. This meant that his plans for the rest of the year—of continuing to Tibet—had to be given up, for he had no means of making observations of altitude.

Hedin had managed to cross one of the worst deserts of the world, but the price he paid was high indeed. Two of the four men who started with him lost their lives, all but one of the camels he bought for the expedition died, and the loss of his instruments and supplies forced him to abandon his plans for the immediate future. There was nothing for him to do but wait until new instruments arrived from Europe, and that was going to take months. The adventure in the desert had been foolhardy, expensive, and totally unproductive of scientific results.

But Hedin never accepted defeat, and over the years his desert adventure turned out to be profitable after all. For many years he was one of the most sought-after lecturers in Central Europe. His travelogues attracted thousands of people, and his lecture on the Takla Makan Desert was one of his most successful presentations. Nearly forty years after the event, he spoke in Detroit to a large audience, describing in detail the slow, torturous progress of his caravan (the "death march," as he called it), and his listeners became so involved in the story that when the lecture was over, everybody rushed to the drinking fountain in the lobby of the auditorium to assuage their thirst. (The writer heard this description of Hedin's lecture, which was given in Detroit in the early 1930s, in 1976, from a member of the audience who still recalled all the details of Hedin's thrilling, death-defying adventure.) Lecturing was one of Hedin's main sources of income for decades, and thus the failure of his desert expedition yielded considerable profit, even if not of a scientific kind.

Hedin returned to his base in Kashgar in late June, 1895, to wait for replacements for his instruments and supplies. To fill the time, he returned once more to the Pamir Highlands. This time, the Pamirs were the scene of intense activity: the surveying and marking of the boundary between British and Russian territories.

High-ranking army officers and top boundary and surveying specialists from both sides, all with large military escorts, camped out there in the summer of 1895, and Hedin's description of the banquets that the two delegations continuously offered each other gives us a glimpse of a forgotten era. The festivities (at which Hedin, as a European visitor, was an honored guest) were attended by British and Russians in full dress uniform and featured entertainment and the best food and drink that Europe could offer, to celebrate the settlement of the two great powers' long-standing rivalry for control of Inner Asia.

In early October, when Hedin returned to Kashgar, he found the new instruments that had been sent from Berlin to replace those lost in the desert. The shipment included barometers, hygrometers, and three loads of supplies as well—clothes, canned foods, tobacco, and so forth. Once more Russia was kind to Hedin: all supplies were forwarded to him free of charge from Saint Petersburg to Kashgar, where he had been the house guest of the Russian consul-general.

After organizing a new caravan, led once again by his faithful servant Islam Bai, Hedin left Kashgar on December 14, 1895, headed for points east. His principal purpose was to explore northern Tibet and eventually reach China's eastern provinces, thence to return home.

The first stop on this new phase of the expedition was the oasis of Khotan, on the southern rim of the Tarim Basin, a place famous since ancient times for its high-quality jade. Hedin's route not only was well trod by local caravans but had been followed on earlier occasions by a number of other European travelers; however, he made up for that by recording detailed data on stream flow, winds, precipitation, and geological formations, as well as information about the size and population of each village. One of his most valuable contributions to our knowledge of the Tarim Basin was a veritable treasure chest of place names, never before recorded so completely. He continued his detailed mapping and compiled the first fully reliable map of the settlements that make up the Khotan oasis.

Early in January, 1896, Hedin was ready to continue his journey.

His aim was to follow the principal stream of the oasis all the way across the desert interior of the Tarim Basin to its northern rim, to the Tarim River. Although he never stated his aim in those terms, he may well have wished to show that not even a desert with as evil a reputation as the Takla Makan could defeat him twice in a row. But before he had started on his journey, he made an excursion to a ruined settlement a few kilometers distant from the town of Khotan. The terra-cotta heads and figurines he found there showed distinct artistic influences that connect the area with India and Persia. A few days later, after he had started in earnest on his intended crossing of the desert, he came across two more ruined settlements. His finds there underlined once more the cosmopolitan character of the past in this area, traversed as it was by trade routes connecting China, India, and the Near East.

Hedin described his finds in his report on the voyage: frescoes, bronzes, and pottery, all bearing unmistakable influences of Indian and, in some instances, Persian art. He was not a trained archaeologist, and he did not pursue the matter beyond reporting the finds and giving their exact locations. Within the next two decades, European archaeologists did excavate these sites, and the results of their labors had an unprecedented impact on our knowledge of Inner Asia's history. Hedin pointed the way; others followed and completed the work.

For several weeks Hedin and his caravan trekked north across the Takla Makan Desert; it was still winter, and enough water was available to provide for the men and their pack animals. It was while in the very center of the desert that Hedin was able to observe at close range one of the rare beasts of Inner Asia, the wild camel. In fact, one of his servants shot one, and Hedin sketched and photographed the animal before it was skinned. He saw to it that the skin was transported to the nearest village, eventually to be shipped back to Sweden.

Finally, in late February, the expedition reached the Tarim. Hedin had proved to his own satisfaction that the desert could not defeat him, even though he had crossed it at its widest north-south extent. He then considered what to do next. He was opposed to returning the way he had come and decided instead to turn east and follow the Tarim River all the way to the mysterious lake where it ended its course, Lop Nor.

The problem of the Lop Nor, or Wandering Lake, as Hedin often called it, interested him during his entire life. He returned to it on more than one occasion, and the behavior of this body of water occupies an important place in his writings.

Two great geographers, Przhevalsky and Richthofen, formulated theories on its shape and location. The most important single fact about this body of water is its changing shape: a glance at Hedin's maps based on his 1896 survey and at the most reliable current maps shows that it changes often and radically. At times it is a string of shallow, salty lakes strung out in a north-south direction, as shown by Hedin in 1896. At other times, as on the most detailed Soviet maps of the 1960s, it is a single, sizable lake, again having its longest dimension along a north-south axis.

Hedin took careful measurements of the streams feeding the Lop Nor lakes—of their breadth and depth and of the speed and volume of the current. In the canoes of the local people, called Loplik (Lop-men), he made several journeys along the shallow waterways connecting the lakes. He described in detail the vegetation of the district, the large areas covered by reeds, and the fishing habits of the natives, and he returned not only with maps and copious notes but with excellent sketches of the district and its people.

By late April, Hedin was ready to return to Khotan, where he had left the bulk of his supplies. His friend Petrovsky, the Russian consul-general in Kashgar, sent a courier to tell him that letters awaited him in Khotan. On his return journey he skirted the southern edge of the desert and arrived in Khotan in late May, 1896.

On his return to Khotan, Hedin heard that the Chinese authorities, through long and careful investigation, had found the men who had stolen the supplies he had left behind on his crossing of the desert a year earlier. Some of his possessions were returned to him, and he had the satisfaction of knowing that the thieves were brought to court and sentenced. Although this did not alter the fact that he had lost a year of travel as a result of the theft, it left him with a better feeling about the adventure, and he was able to spend a month of rest in the house of one of Khotan's wealthy merchants, which was put at his disposal by command of the local Chinese governor.

By late June, he had assembled a new caravan, headed once again by the faithful Islam Bai, and on June 29 he left Khotan, bound for the highlands of northern Tibet. He had eight attendants, as he referred to them. They were local people, including a Chinese interpreter, and one of the men had already traveled through the region as a servant of other Europeans.

Hedin had purchased six camels, twenty-one horses, and twenty-nine donkeys to carry supplies. When, after a journey of nearly two months through the high northern rim of Tibet, he first reached an encampment of Mongol nomads, only three camels, three horses, and one donkey had survived the journey. Traveling at high altitudes that often exceeded 4,000 meters was hard on people, too. Hedin's Chinese interpreter became so ill with altitude sickness that he had to be returned to Khotan, and even Islam Bai became seriously ill. In spite of the hardships he and his caravan had to endure, Hedin managed to cope with it all. His luck held. The one thing he dreaded most, an infection of his eye, did not return, and he seems to have ended the trip in better condition than his servants.

The journey led through regions recently explored by other Europeans, but Hedin managed, following Richthofen's advice, to gather more information on climate, geology, and animal life. He also kept up his rigorous mapping, and at the end of each day he transferred the observations about distances and direction to a set of sketch maps that he could convert into detailed and accurate maps when he returned to Europe.

Hedin was always interested in wildlife. This time, his men shot both wild asses and wild yaks, and he was able to make detailed drawings of these animals at close range. The journey itself tended to be monotonous and difficult; they crossed the ranges through high passes and traveled mostly through uninhabited country. Twice he crossed one of the principal ranges of northern Tibet, the Arka Tagh (part of the Kunlun range, and now called the Przhevalsky Mountains), and passed a long chain of isolated salt lakes, always pressing eastward, toward China. Though it was still autumn, the air was cold, and the night temperatures were below freezing. Finally, on the first of October, after traveling for fifty-five days without encountering a single human being, they met a Mongol family. The worst of the trip was over. They were able to get some fresh food and some rest, and they bought pack horses to continue the journey.

The Mongols whose encampment provided this welcome change were hunters and pastoralists. Hedin took advantage of the few days he spent in their camp to start learning Mongolian, a new language that was to serve him well on this and later journeys. The Mongols he met then and later as he traveled eastward were hospitable folk, accepting him at their campfires and offering him and his men both sheep's milk and fermented mare's milk.

The journey took Hedin and his servants across the Tsaidam Basin, part of the Chinese-Tibetan borderlands, past the lake the Mongols called Koko Nor, and on November 15 they reached the small town of Tenkar in the Chinese province of Tsinghai. Today a railroad connects the area with the rest of China, but in 1896 it was the far west of the country. An inquiry to the local governor directed the small caravan to the house of a missionary couple, the Reinhards. The husband was Dutch, the wife American. Hedin recalled that she asked him, " 'Do you speak English?' I told her, 'Yes, I thought so,' and very soon our tongues were going at express speed." She was the first Westerner Hedin had met since he had left Kashgar ten months earlier.

Tenkar was a stopping place for the embassy that the Dalai Lama, the priestly ruler of Tibet, sent to Peking every three years with a tribute to the emperor of China. At the time, the journey from the Tibetan capital, Lhasa, to Peking took five months, with a long rest at Tenkar. Hedin met the head of the embassy, a high-ranking lama, and through hard bargaining bought from him a precious porcelain cup, a silk shawl, a prayer drum, and other objects that were supposed to have been part of the tribute to the emperor.

Hedin's next stop was Hsi-ning, the capital of Tsinghai province, where he spent a week as a guest of English missionaries. There he dismissed all his servants except Islam Bai, paying them well and presenting them with the surviving horses of the caravan to return to their homes in the distant Tarim Basin. He was now on his way back, but it took him another three months to reach Peking. On the way he stopped to visit temples and monasteries and make sketches of towns and people, and on March 2, 1897, he saw the great city wall of Peking in the distance.

He was going to find a hotel when he saw two Cossacks standing guard at the entrance of a large compound. Upon inquiry he found that it was the Russian embassy. The Russian chargé d'affaires received him with open arms; he had had word from Saint Petersburg that Hedin was on his way to Peking and had reserved a suite of rooms for his stay in the capital.

After a few days' rest, Hedin had to decide on his return route to Sweden. He could have sailed across the Pacific to Canada or the United States and thence to Europe, or he could have taken a steamer home by way of India, the Suez Canal, and the Mediterranean. He chose a route that seemed shorter but was much more demanding than the others and returned home by way of Mongolia, Siberia, and Saint Petersburg. At that time the Trans-Siberian Railroad was not yet completed, and he had to travel by carriage from Peking across Mongolia to the Russian border.

Once more, the Russian government offered every kind of help Hedin could have desired. The Russian embassy in Peking shipped his trunks and cases back to Sweden free of charge and provided him with a mounted escort of two Russian cossacks to the Russian border. Hedin traveled to the town of Kalgan, a short distance northwest of Peking, to start on the long road to the Russian railhead nearly three thousand kilometers to the west, at Kansk in Siberia.

Travel across northwest China and Mongolia was by means of what foreigners called a "Peking car," a simple conveyance with a roof and canvas sides but no springs, drawn by four Mongols mounted on small ponies. In order to endure what Hedin called "a true instrument of torture," he stuffed all manner of blankets and cushions and a mattress inside the carriage to absorb the shocks when it hit ruts and rocks while being dragged along at top speed. After several weeks of hard travel he reached the town of Urga, now the capital of Outer Mongolia and renamed Ulan Bator. The snow on the ground was too deep for the ponies, and he switched to slower—and steadier—camels to continue his journey to the Russian border. There, at the town of Kyakhta, he changed his conveyance to a sled drawn, in the Russian manner, by three horses (1953, 175–79).

Siberia was still covered by deep snow, and at Lake Baikal, Siberia's largest lake and the world's deepest, to Hedin's astonishment the sled continued westward on the ice; during the winter months, a post station was maintained on the lake itself. There were fresh horses, and the weary traveler could refresh himself with tea from the samovar in the station.

At long last, Hedin reached the railroad at Kansk in Central Siberia and at the beginning of May arrived in Saint Petersburg. At his request, the Swedish legation arranged for him to have an audience with Tsar Nicholas II. In his memoirs, *Great Men and Kings,* Hedin provides an interesting protrait of the tsar, dressed Russian fashion in a red shirt, blue breeches, and high boots, sitting and talking in his study at his winter residence of Tsarskoe Selo (now Pushkin), near Saint Petersburg. Russia had a vital interest in Inner Asia, and the tsar was well informed about the area, having read the reports of the Russian explorers who had traveled there during the past three decades (1950, 1:234–39).

Nicholas II asked Hedin to mark his itinerary on a map, quizzed him at length on the suitability of the newly drawn British-Russian frontier in the Pamirs, and agreed to have the Russian edition of Hedin's book on the expedition dedicated to him. He then asked Hedin whether he intended to return to Inner Asia and added, "Let me know when you are ready for your next expedition. Perhaps I can help in some way."

With that tantalizing promise on his mind, Hedin took his leave, returned to Saint Petersburg, and on May 10, 1897, landed in Stockholm after an absence of more than three years. His family was delighted to have him back safe and sound after his many adventures, and right away he got down to the task of writing reports on this, his first scientific expedition.

Even taking into account the fact that Hedin had sent a steady stream of letters home describing his work and his travels in detail from day to day and had kept voluminous notes in addition to the maps, panoramas, and sketches he made, the speed with which he wrote his books is astonishing. The first version of his report of the 1893–97 expedition, which was published in Swedish and took up two volumes with a total of almost 1,100 printed pages, appeared less than a year after his return to Sweden. Complete translations of the book into Russian, German, and English appeared within eighteen months after the original version. The book, entitled *Through Asia* in the English translation, was an instant success and made Hedin's name practically a household word among not only geographers all over the western world but the general public as well.

But Hedin also had scientific ambitions. The popular report on the 1893–97 expedition brought in much-needed funds: when he arrived in Peking in March, 1897, Hedin had no money left and had borrowed funds for his return journey to Sweden. Writing popular books was lucrative and necessary. On the other hand, Hedin also felt that preparing reports on the scientific results of his expeditions was expected of him.

During his stays at the Russian consulate in Kashgar he had already written several short articles, and these were published in Swedish, German, and English geographical journals. Now, back at his desk in Stockholm, he worked on his popular book and at the same time on a report to the scientific community. The scientific report was published in 1900, less than a year after the two large volumes on his travels were first published in Sweden. Entitled "The Geographic-Scientific Results of My Travels in Central Asia, 1894–97," it was presented to the world of geographers in what was then the most prestigious geographical journal in the world, *Petermann's Mitteilungen,* in Germany. The journal devoted an entire issue of its famous special or supplementary volumes to Hedin's report.

The volume consists of 400 closely packed pages in fine print, most of it written by Hedin, with short articles on special problems by well-known scholars from Sweden, Germany, and England. The scientific report may be described as a carefully edited abstract of the popular work published earlier in Stockholm, with most of the details about people and adventures omitted; it adhered closely to observed facts. Reading it, one gets the impression that the author kept detailed field notebooks and entered in them a variety of observations on rocks, streams, animals, settlement patterns, modes of farming, and irrigation. Little escaped his notice, and the reader is overwhelmed by detail.

A good example of Hedin's approach to a scientific report is chapter five of the publication, entitled "Northern Tibet." The author fills forty-five pages with detailed observations on streams, lakes, soil, rock materials, and animal life. A two-page summary at the end of the chapter reports the height of passes he crossed and the general directions of the ranges as he observed them, without attempting to fit his observations into a wider frame, and offers his views on the place and importance of the range he followed for nearly two months, the Arka Tagh.

One exception to the general tenor of Hedin's scientific report is the chapter dealing with the problem of the Wandering Lake, Lop Nor. There, Hedin clearly encountered a real problem, as evidenced by conflicting reports issued by Chinese, Russian, and German observers. He provides a full translation of an early-nineteenth-century Chinese report on the lake, compares his own observations with those made by Jesuit astronomers of the eighteenth century who traversed the region while in the service of the Chinese government, and offers his own hypothesis on the deplacements of Lop Nor as a result of changes in stream flow and the effect of winds.

Thomas Holdich, a prominent English geographer of the time, described Hedin's mapping of Lop Nor as "one of the most valuable of modern additions to the geography of Central Asia" (Holdich 1899, 162), a well-earned tribute to the one important scientific contribution Hedin made to the subject during his expedition.

The 1899 report on scientific results is illustrated by a set of detailed maps on a scale of one to one million compiled by the famous German mapmaking establishment of Justus Perthes, in Gotha, which published *Petermann's Mitteilungen*. The maps show Hedin's own itinerary, compiled from 550 map sheets that in turn represent the clean copy of the sketch maps he made while he was actually riding on the trail on horseback or camelback. Accurate measurement of the maps shows, wrote the German cartographer who prepared the printed maps, that Hedin traveled 10,500 kilometers in 1894–97, the equivalent of one-quarter of the earth's circumference. The figure is impressive. Yet, on close examination of the maps, one is struck by the fact that with the exception of the Lop Nor district, Hedin made significant contributions in his maps only in his crossings of the Takla Makan Desert. On his journey along the northern rim of Tibet he followed a relatively easy route, and the topographic details of the mountain ranges he observed along the way were taken, as the German cartographer indicates, from the work of other European explorers, French, British, Russian, and German.

The botanical results of the expedition were slim and covered a total of only five printed pages in the report. One part of the report that does retain a lasting value is Hedin's gazetteer of geographical names from the Tarim Basin. Vámbéry, the Hungarian orientalist who a few years earlier had written the preface to Hedin's first book, published an article on the subject in the early 1890s, but Hedin's twenty-page, closely printed list of place names, most of them translated into German, remains a very valuable contribution to the geography of Inner Asia.

VII

The Second Expedition, 1899–1902

Hedin's family and close friends say that during the early years of his career the time he spent at home was devoted to two things: getting the results of the latest voyage into print and searching for funds to finance the next expedition. The year 1898 and the first half of 1899 were indeed devoted to writing up the results of the expedition of 1893–97. But this was also a time when his work was being recognized; honors were showered on him even before the results of the expedition appeared in print.

Within less than six months after his return to Stockholm, the Geographical Society of Berlin honored him with the Carl Ritter medal, established to recognize "a first—and successful—pioneering expedition." The following year, 1898, he received the Founder's Medal of the Royal Geographical Society of Great Britain, the Grand Prize of the Geographical Society of Paris, and the Hauer Medal of the Geographical Society of Vienna. But the honor he treasured most came from his native Sweden.

On April 24, 1898, eighteen years after the day when Hedin as a teenager had watched the triumphal return of Nordenskiöld from his discovery of the Northeast Passage, he was the guest of honor at a formal dinner held in Stockholm's Grand Hotel. After dinner, Nordenskiöld spoke first, expressed his pleasure that the Vega Medal, the highest honor offered by the Swedish Geographical Society, was being presented to a fellow Swede, and handed the medal to King Oscar II, who gave it to Hedin. Hedin received many more medals and honors during his long life, but none meant as much to him as the Vega Medal, which was given to him in the presence of the man who inspired him to become an explorer.

By June, 1899, Hedin was ready to return to Central Asia. The results of his previous journey had been published, and he had gathered enough financial support to undertake an even more ambitious one. King Oscar contributed support from his private fortune, and that royal gesture inspired other Swedes to help Hedin. Emanuel Nobel's contribution was the most important of those private donations.

There was also support from another source. On his return from Asia in 1897, Hedin had had an audience with tsar Nicholas II. On that occasion the tsar had promised him help with his next expedition. In April, 1899, Hedin went to Saint Petersburg and had another audience with the tsar. That time, Nicholas offered him an escort of twenty-four cossacks for his expedition. Hedin replied that his lack of experience in leading such a group and his concern lest his status as a private citizen and explorer might be cast in doubt if he were to appear at the head of such an armed escort forced him to refuse this generous offer. The tsar understood and agreed with Hedin's suggestion that the escort be limited to four cossacks and promised to give an order to that effect to the minister of war, General Kuropatkin.

As Hedin was about to take his leave, the tsar said:

Please send me a letter from time to time, to let me know how your expedition is faring, and give me your opinion of the Cossacks. I have a lively interest in keeping posted both on your and their doings, and hope to see you here on your return. (1950, 1:239–41)

The following day Hedin was summoned to the office of the minister of war. General Kuropatkin discussed the composition of the escort with him; Hedin requested that two of the cossacks be Buddhists of Mongol origin and the two others Russian Orthodox. Hedin was planning to enter Tibet, a Buddhist country, and having Buddhists in his party would serve his purpose very well.

Imperial favor shown to Hedin extended to other aspects of the expedition. He was carrying a large number of trunks and boxes with him, some twenty-two in all, packed with instruments, equipment, books, maps, and food, and all this was shipped by the

Russian government to the Russian railroad terminus in Central Asia free of charge. And when Hedin, having traveled by rail from Saint Petersburg to the Caspian Sea, then crossed by ferry to its eastern shore and was about to start on the last leg of his railroad trip, he found a private car at his disposition, complete with sitting room, bedroom, and shower.

When Hedin arrived at the end of the railroad, deep in the mountains of Russian Central Asia, he found his faithful caravan leader Islam Bai waiting for him; around his neck Islam Bai wore with pride the gold medallion King Oscar had sent him in recognition of his services to Hedin. In the town of Osh, the railroad terminal, Hedin once more experienced trouble with his eye; while recuperating, he stayed two weeks as the house guest of the Russian military commander of the district. Finally, on July 31, 1899, he left Osh with a small caravan, crossed the Pamirs, and on August 16 arrived in Kashgar at the friendly compound of the Russian consul-general.

Kashgar was a crossroads of Central Asia; during Hedin's three weeks' stay at the Russian consulate, travelers from England and France passed through. There was also regular mail service between Kashgar, the Russian territories west of the Pamirs, and European Russia, and it was through the good offices of Petrovsky, the consul-general, that Hedin received mail from home during the next two years.

Hedin's first goal was to make a journey down the Tarim River as far as its terminal lake, Lop Nor. He had a small boat built in the shape of a floating platform, 10.5 meters long and 2.5 meters wide. On it he had a small tent, a portable darkroom where he developed photographic plates, a cookstove, his bed, and room for his boatmen. Once more, as he had done on his desert journey, he measured a base line along the riverbank of 1,250 meters and determined how long the boat took to cover it. Having thus established an average speed for the boat of a little less than three kilometers per hour, he was able to make a continuous map of the river; this was the principal objective of this "journey by boat through the desert," as he referred to it in his book.

Europeans had traveled across the Tarim Basin many times

during the previous thirty years, but no accurate map of the river had ever been prepared. At the end of the journey Hedin could say that "no river outside Europe has been mapped with the same degree of minuteness and accuracy" (1903, 1:85). And it was a very pleasant way to travel compared with riding horses or camels. He observed the riverbanks, the wildlife, and the character of the immediate vicinity of the stream, took hundreds of measurements of stream flow, volume, and speed, and entered notes on the vegetation and settlements on the banks. The natives would bring sheep and chicken whenever the boat stopped, and in this manner Hedin floated down the Tarim for two-and-a-half months while the rest of his caravan followed regular routes to their meeting place at the lower end of the river.

On December 7, 1899, the river journey came to an end. Hedin set up a base camp in the eastern end of the Tarim Basin and got his equipment ready, planning to cross the basin to its southern edge. It was in this remote corner of Inner Asia that he met a fellow explorer, Charles Bonin, a Frenchman who had come to the area from China, following old routes toward the Lop Nor. The two Europeans spent the day together; Bonin then turned back east toward China, while Hedin, leaving his base camp in charge of one of the cossacks, who was to take weather observations during his absence, turned south toward the Cherchen River.

Hedin retraced his route of 1897, found that his measurements of distance were accurate to within half a mile over a route of 177 miles, spent a lonely Christmas, and returned to his base camp on January 15, 1900. By that time, the two Siberian cossacks arrived, having traveled on horseback from their distant garrison. These two were Buryat Mongols, Buddhists, who were to accompany him on his journey to Tibet.

The next months Hedin spent in the Lop Nor area, making surveys, observing the local inhabitants, and getting ready for the journey across the mountains that guard the southern edge of the Tarim Basin into Tibet. One June 30, Hedin sent two of the cossacks back to Kashgar with mail to be forwarded to Europe and set out to cross the Arka Tagh into Tibet. Once across that high range, Hedin writes, "we had . . . plunged into a region which was an absolute *terra incognita*, except that I should cross my own former route, Wellby's, Rockhill's, and Bonvalot's each at a single point" (1903, 1:513). He was excited to know that he and his party "were the first human beings to tread those mountains where there existed no path, where there never had been a path, and where there was not a footprint visible, except those made by the hoof of yak, antelope, or kulan [a wild ass]" (1903, 1:513).

Hedin loved to believe that he was a true discoverer of places never before seen by human beings. He ignored not only the fact that the native inhabitants of these regions had wandered over the same terrain for many centuries before his arrival, but that other explorers, Europeans, had crisscrossed the high plateau of Tibet before him. Technically the statement quoted above may well have been correct, and by touching on areas where others had made observations before him he only followed Richthofen's advice, hoping that his sketch maps, photographs, drawings, and panoramas would be superior to those of fellow Europeans who had been there before him.

For four months Hedin wandered around northern Tibet and then returned to his base camp at Temirlik, on the lower Tarim, in October. After a thorough rest, he resumed his travels across the area surrounding Lop Nor and in March, 1901, found the ruins of an ancient city, Lou Lan. He discovered ruined houses and gathered a substantial number of artifacts, including wooden statues and Chinese writings on both wooden tablets and strips of paper. The archaeologists to whom Hedin sent these objects established their age as the second, third, and fourth centuries of the Christian era. Lou Lan was an important outpost on the route from China to Central Asia, and contemporary Chinese sources as well as the reports of Chinese pilgrims following the route toward India in the fifth and seventh centuries A.D. underline its importance.

Hedin completed his spring journeys by surveying both the "old" and the "new" Lop Nor and returned to his base camp at the beginning of April, 1901. There he acquired the services of a Mongol priest; got himself a complete Mongol costume—robe, hat, boots; shaved his head and mustache; and smeared his face with grease, soot, and a brown dye. "After the concoction had dried my complexion became a dirty gray" (1903, 2:304). He decided to take only a small caravan with him, hid his compass and barometer in the voluminous pockets of his Mongol robe, put his camera and plates in the baggage, sent his faithful servant Islam Bai back to Kashgar with the rest of his baggage, and on May 17, 1901, left his camp accompanied by one of the Buryat Mongol cossacks, the Mongol priest, and four servants. Both Hedin and the cossack were disguised as pilgrims, but that was of little avail. Once on Tibetan soil, they were met on August 5 by a Tibetan official who knew that a "Swedish European" was on his way to the holy city of Lhasa, the capital of Tibet.

Hedin and his companions were told to wait at their encampment. Four days later the local governor arrived carrying explicit orders. "You will not go to Lhasa. You will not go another day, not another step, towards Lhasa. If you do, you will lose your heads" (1903, 2:379). Hedin tried to argue, asking that a message be sent to Lhasa asking for permission for him to go to the holy city, but it was in vain.

The Tibetans, nominally under Chinese sovereignty, were very much masters of their own remote realm. They were aware that Tibet controlled the northern approaches to India and thus represented a potential menace to British rule there. They were anxious to keep their country out of the possible sphere of British influence. When Hedin tried despite the governor's threat to head toward the Tibetan capital, the Tibetan official who stopped him called him Sahib, the title given to the British in India. In vain did Hedin protest that he was not British. Though he was within two hundred kilometers of Lhasa, he was not allowed to visit the holy city. He finally gave up and turned westward to reach the British-controlled province of Ladakh.

In retrospect and in light of the substantial scientific results Hedin obtained in his 1899–1902 expedition, not being able to reach Lhasa was really a minor setback. Lhasa, the holy city, long forbidden to Europeans, had been his goal, he had failed to achieve it, and his frustration was intense. But that did not lessen the importance of his expedition's scientific achievements.

On his return journey through western Tibet, Hedin followed

closely the route taken six years earlier by Littledale, an English explorer, and arrived in Leh, Ladakh's capital, on December 29, 1901.

There was mail waiting for him there, including funds to support his trip home and an invitation from Lord Curzon, viceroy of India, to visit him in Calcutta. On January 1, 1902, Hedin started out on horseback from Leh to Kashmir, thence to Lahore, and by rail to Calcutta.

Curzon was a geographer by training and had a lively interest in Central Asia. Hedin was received as a most welcome visitor, and during his stay at the viceregal residence discussed his journeys with his host.

Instead of returning home by ship, Hedin and one of the two cossacks who accompanied him to India returned to Russian territory by way of Ladakh and Kashgar, and thence to Saint Petersburg. He met with the tsar, reported to him on his journey, and thanked him for the many favors extended by the Russian government. Finally, on June 27, 1902, he landed in Stockholm and was reunited with his family.

A few hours after his arrival a high court official came with greetings from King Oscar II and a handwritten letter from the sovereign. He wrote:

In haste, Welcome! I am delighted to bestow on you a well-deserved title of nobility, a "welcome home," as it were. Think about it and let Count Rosen know by Tuesday what title you wish to have. Your friend, Oscar. (1950, 1:239–41)

When Hedin appeared for an audience with the king, he asked to keep his name. It was in that form, Sven Anders Hedin, that the patent of nobility was written, the last bestowed by the king of Sweden. Hedin's coat of arms shows a blue hemisphere on a gold shield, with a map of Asia. Three small shells, the pilgrims' symbol, are above, and the motto "Voluntate et labore" (with a will and hard work) is below.

His elevation to the nobility seemed perfectly logical to Hedin. His hero, Nordenskiöld, had been created a baron of the realm in

1880, while the commander of the *Vega,* Nordenskiöld's ship, was given a title of nobility. Hedin was unaware of the strong trend toward a more democratic society that was already evident in Sweden, and this was the first of many occasions when his countrymen objected to his obsession with honors and titles. As far as he was concerned, he had earned the honor bestowed upon him by his sovereign.

Within a year of Hedin's return from his 1899–1902 expedition, the Swedish original of his book on the voyage, two volumes totaling 1,367 printed pages, was published. Complete or partial translations of the work in Danish, German, English, French, Italian, Russian, Spanish, Czech, and Hungarian appeared within three years. Hedin was without a doubt one of the most widely known—and widely read—explorers of his time.

Critical acclaim for his book on the expedition came quickly. A few months after the publication of the English translation, Hedin was awarded the Victoria Medal of the Royal Geographical Society of London, a medal instituted "for the highest record of geographical research." In a review of the English version published in the society's journal, the work was described as "the best book of travel since Palgrave's *Arabia*" (*Geographical Journal* 23[1904]: 116).

But Hedin always felt the obligation to publish not only travel books but scientific results of his expeditions as well. Between 1904 and 1907, all but one small part of the results of the 1899–1902 expedition were published. The first four volumes of the report, entitled *Scientific Results of a Journey in Central Asia, 1899–1902,* were written by Hedin himself; parts 1 and 2 of the fifth volume and parts 1, 2, and 3 of the sixth were prepared by specialists.

The sheer mass of Hedin's writings published in these volumes is overwhelming: 2,487 printed pages, in a large format. These four volumes also include 217 full-page reproductions of his photographs, 1,588 smaller photographs and drawings, and 75 maps and panoramas. The scientific results may be divided into three sections: two volumes dealing with the Tarim River and Lop Nor, two volumes dealing with several sections of Tibet, and the album of drawings of people from Western and Central Asia.

There is no doubt about the significance of Hedin's study of the Tarim River. His detailed description of the several segments of its course, from the point on the upper river where he launched his raft all the way to the delta, is accompanied by drawings and photographs, by detailed studies of the course of the river and its oxbows and meanders, and by a mass of valuable hydrographic data. These data include breadth, depth, and velocity of the river and the relationship of the Tarim and its tributaries, all unknown before Hedin's river journey. He also included an important discussion of the formation and movements of sand dunes in the desert adjoining the river.

The volume entitled *Lop Nor* is based on surveys Hedin carried out during his several journeys around this wandering lake. His work is, in essence, an attempt to explain the displacements of this body of water through recent centuries, displacements illustrated by maps made by the Chinese, who had controlled the area during its recent history, and by foreign travelers. Hedin's explanation, which he felt was the best he could make at the time, states that

> since the whole area is at the same level, hydrographical distribution must be extremely sensitive to any change in level. There are two constant factors effecting such changes, namely the eastern sandstorms, which are especially violent in the spring, filling the basin and pressing the lake westward, and the sediment carried down by the river. (1904–7, 2:265)

Hedin included in his report complete details of the leveling he undertook in the Lop Nor area and provided an excellent "vegetation and physiographic map of the Cherchen and Lop deserts," showing water, steppe, sand, clay, scree, and forest. The "pendulum-like oscillations of the terminal lake of the Tarim system" (1904–7, 2:plate 40) are fully illustrated on a map showing the Tarim as it appeared on old Chinese maps, its present maximum extent, its old westernmost and abandoned bed, its present easternmost bed, the present lake called the Kara Koshun, and the extent of the entire Lop Nor depression.

In a separate map, plate 57 of the second volume of the reports, Hedin presented a physiographic diagram of the Tarim
Basin, with an overlay showing the catchment areas of the streams
draining into the East Turkestan Basin and their extent in square
kilometers. This map retains its value and stands as one of
Hedin's outstanding contributions to the geography of Central
Asia.

Throughout his journey on the Tarim, Hedin collected a vast
array of measurements on nearly all aspects of the hydrography
of the river. These statistics provide a complete profile of an
unusually interesting exotic river that has its source outside a
desert, traverses a large desert area, and receives added quantities
of water from the surrounding mountains.

In the last part of the volume entitled *Lop Nor,* Hedin includes
material dealing with the history and the people of the area.
There are population statistics of East Turkestan, the term used
to distinguish the Tarim Basin from the Russian-controlled West
Turkestan, the desert area lying west of the Pamirs. There is a
population map of the area and an excellent gazetteer that goes
beyond the place-name list published as a result of his preceding
journey. It not only lists place names but identifies each one,
whether it be that of a river bed, an inhabited tract, a spring, a
ridge, a group of bushes, or any other object.

Together, the first two volumes of *Scientific Results of a Journey
in Central Asia, 1899–1902* represent an important and lasting
contribution to the geography of the area. The third and fourth
volumes deal, respectively, with North and East Tibet and Central
and West Tibet. The review of the work published in the *Geographical Journal* of the Royal Geographical Society of London
provides a good summary judgment in saying that "the title 'Scientific Results' is misleading. They contain, rather, the profuse
detail from which results may be condensed." In the words of that
review, one must "record admiration for the endurance, physical
and mental, which is attested first by the exploration involved,
and next by the preparation of its results" (*Geographical Journal* 27
[1906]: 613). These volumes, like the popular report published
earlier, are descriptive, not analytical.

In the volume entitled *Central and West Tibet,* Hedin included, for the first time in his career, several chapters dealing with the journeys of other men who traveled in the area before him: Russians, English, French, and the Indian surveyors, called "pundits," who were trained by the Survey of India to work in areas inaccessible to Europeans.

More important is Hedin's attempt, in the concluding chapters of this volume, to set forth, again for the first time, his thoughts about the main lines of the relief of Inner Asia, under the titles "Orography of the Tibetan Highlands" and "Hypsometry and Relief of the Tibetan Plateau." Later, in the volumes reporting on his last expedition before the First World War, Hedin returned to this theme, refining his earlier observations.

The fifth volume of *Scientific Results* contains very valuable material: detailed meteorological, geodetic, and astronomical observations Hedin made during his journey, presented in summary form by two collaborators, Nils Ekholm and K. G. Olsson. The sixth volume consists of four parts; the last of these, on archaeological results of the expedition, did not appear until 1920, but the first three parts were published between 1904 and 1907.

Part 1 of the sixth volume, written by the zoologist W. Leche, is a brief analysis, sixty-nine pages long, of zoological specimens collected by Hedin. Part 2 of the volume is an attempt to present in summary form the notations Hedin made on surface geology along his route. It was written by H. Backström and H. Johansson.

The third part of volume 6 is entitled "Racial Types from Western and Central Asia." It consists of a four-page introduction by Hedin and 86 plates containing 271 drawings—a selection from Hedin's work as an artist starting with his first journey to Baku and Persia in 1886 and ending with drawings made in 1899–1902. It is hard to judge this album of sketches as "scientific results" compared with the analyses of the Tarim River and Lop Nor. The collection consists of both the first simple drawings of a twenty year old with little artistic training and the outstanding portraits made years later by an accomplished graphic artist. Many years later, in 1964, a special exhibition of Hedin's drawings was held in Stockholm, and a memorial volume, *Sven Hedin as an Artist,* was published on that occasion. As a retrospective, that exhibition and the book containing excerpts from it were fully justified. But the volume *Racial Types* does not really belong among the scientific results of a voyage of exploration. It represents an artist's pride in his own achievement but has no particular scientific value, devoid as it is of any commentary on its significance.

VIII

First Encounter with World Affairs, 1905

Hedin remained in Europe from mid-1903 to the fall of 1905. He wrote a detailed popular account of his journey and assembled materials for the publication of the scientific results of his voyage. The Swedish Parliament gave him a substantial grant toward the publication costs of the scientific results, but the size of the work far exceeded his expectations. The funds ran out, and in order to make sure the entire set of volumes would be published, Hedin gave a series of lecture tours all over Europe to earn enough money for printing costs.

The years 1903–5 were eventful ones in Europe and in Asia. Three events in particular involved Hedin and introduced new dimensions into his life, a concern with world affairs and an intense commitment to the welfare of Sweden. That commitment was to create for Hedin a reputation as a participant in international affairs, making him a political figure of importance in Sweden.

The three events were the Russo-Japanese War of 1904–5, the British invasion of Tibet in 1904, and the constitutional crisis that resulted in the breakup of the United Kingdom of Sweden and Norway in 1905.

Even though it ended in Russia's defeat, the Russo-Japanese War meant to Hedin that Russia's expansionist tendencies, stopped in the Pacific, might turn westward to secure an outlet to the Atlantic Ocean across northern Sweden and northern Norway. In a few years' time, Hedin was to become the chief Swedish propagandist opposing Russia and calling for Swedish rearmament.

The British invasion of Tibet, in the spring and summer of 1904, was precipitated by British suspicions that Russia was at-

71

tempting to secure a diplomatic foothold in Tibet and possibly a military one. In 1900 and 1901 a Buryat Mongol, Dorcheff, had appeared in Russia, stating that he was a representative of the Dalai Lama. While Dorcheff's credentials were not fully satisfactory and his mission doubtful, the possibility of actual Russian intervention in Tibet aroused a strong British reaction.

The outcome of the British invasion of Tibet was fully predictable: superior British arms and organization broke down Tibetan opposition, and British forces occupied Lhasa for a short time. Hedin felt that this was unprovoked aggression by a great power against a weak and small country. In an article published by a leading German weekly, he objected strongly to the British move. At the time the article was being published, he wrote in the same vein to the viceroy of India, Lord Curzon, who two years earlier had received him in Calcutta and entertained him as a guest in his home. Curzon replied, saying that he understood Hedin's feelings about the Tibetans, but that "as the guardian of India I cannot afford to see Russian influence paramount in Lhasa and I have intervened to prevent it" (June 9, 1904).

British-Russian relations were not too friendly at the time, and Hedin was attacked by several English newspapers that accused him of being a Russian agent. The continuing Russian support of his expeditions and his personal contact with Tsar Nicholas II only gave further strength to the accusation. This time, Lord Curzon wrote Hedin:

> For my own part I have never suspected you of being a Russian agent. Geography is the most cosmopolitan of sciences, and you are the most cosmopolitan of men. But you are a scientist before anything else—the man who more than any other has shown with what resources a great explorer ought to be equipped and what so equipped he ought to accomplish. I hope therefore in the interest of the world that you will perform one more big journey before you settle down. From this point of view I am almost ashamed of having destroyed the virginity of the bride to whom you aspired, viz. Lhasa. (November 13, 1904)

Hedin's strong protest against British action in Tibet was noted not only in the British press but in government circles as well, and quite predictably left some high officials in London opposed to his further plans for exploration in Inner Asia.

The third event of 1904–5, the Swedish-Norwegian crisis, was mainly an internal affair of the two nations involved. It was noted in the world press, however, and Hedin's involvement in it made him a political figure for the first time, while also establishing a close link between Hedin and the future king of Sweden, Crown Prince Gustav.

Sweden and Norway had become united under a single sovereign in 1814, as a result of the complex alliances and treaties of the Napoleonic era. It was a "personal union": the two countries retained their own constitutions, separate parliaments, and separate governments. Only matters of national defense and foreign affairs came under joint administration, and these were dominated by Sweden.

It was the issue of foreign affairs that triggered the crisis of 1905. Norway insisted that its worldwide shipping and commercial interests demanded a separate Norwegian consular service staffed by Norwegians and not controlled by Sweden. Quickly, the entire relationship was questioned, and the crisis was noticed by the world press. On March 25, 1905, the London *Times* published a letter written by the best-known Norwegian of the time, the great polar explorer Fridtjof Nansen.

In his letter Nansen appealed to the world at large for support of the Norwegian cause and contrasted Norwegian democracy with Swedish aristocracy. Needless to say, the letter was not well received in Sweden, and the Swedish government sought ways of putting its views in the best possible light before world opinion.

The day after Nansen's letter was published in the *Times*, the British minister in Stockholm, Sir James Rennell Rodd, gave a formal dinner honoring the recent engagement of Prince Gustav Adolf of Sweden, oldest son of Crown Prince Gustav, to Princess Margaret of England. Among the guests at the dinner was Hedin. Both he and Rennell Rodd told the story in their memoirs. Rennell Rodd wrote:

There was at that time a feeling in Stockholm that we in England were in danger of hearing only one side of the issue with Norway. Nansen had exposed the Norwegian case very fully in the *Times* and, owing to the great popularity which he enjoyed in the British Empire, it was believed that his statement would undoubtedly have a strong influence in moulding opinion there. On the other hand Nansen was regarded by some Swedes as having omitted to mention certain matters which were pertinent to their point of view, and to have drawn conclusions which they considered should not pass unnoticed. (Rennell Rodd 1925, 57–58)

After dinner, Crown Prince Gustav, the Swedish foreign minister, Eric Trolle, the British minister, and Sven Hedin met in a room at the British legation to discuss the crisis. Rennell Rodd pointed out that

as . . . official representative I could do nothing and must obviously maintain an attitude of strict impartiality. But I ventured to suggest that they also had a famous explorer, whose name was as well known to my countrymen as that of Nansen. Why should they not get Sven Hedin to enter the lists and break a lance. (Rennell Rodd 1925, 57–58)

Hedin accepted the charge. As soon as the text of Nansen's letter to the *Times* arrived in Stockholm, he and Foreign Minister Trolle sat down and composed a reply to Nansen's accusations. A retired Swedish diplomat translated the statement into English, and the text was cabled as a letter, signed by Hedin, to London. It appeared in the *Times* on March 29, 1905. Overnight Hedin became a spokesman for his country in one of its major crises.

It was a new role for the man who, although interested in world affairs and certainly committed to the welfare of his country, had made his name over the preceding twenty-five years as an explorer of Inner Asia. But he was asked to do so by the crown prince of Sweden, soon to assume the crown under the name Gustav V; furthermore, at the time of the crisis the crown prince

74

was acting as lieutenant of the realm, standing in for his father, Oscar II, during the king's illness. Hedin liked his new role, and for the next forty years continued to maintain close contact with Gustav V. More than once, in matters domestic and international, Gustav V listened to Hedin's views and entrusted him with important matters both at home and abroad.

By June, 1905, the Swedish-Norwegian constitutional crisis came to a head. On June 12 the Norwegian parliament declared the personal union with Sweden dissolved, and in the fall of 1905 the matter was formally acknowledged in the treaty of Karlstad. Hedin, writing to his German publisher and friend, Albert Brockhaus, stated his views on the crisis.

> I greet the dissolution of this unhappy marriage with honest joy, but Norway's future is fateful and perilous. Russia needs ports on the Atlantic, especially now after the unlucky war with Japan. It is a great advantage to Sweden not to have to defend Norway any longer. (1942, 64)

IX

The Third Expedition, 1906–8

It was October, 1905. Hedin was restless, ready to embark on yet another voyage to the heart of Asia. He had written books on his previous voyage, had assembled a number of observations with a distinct scientific value, and was better known as a traveler than any of his contemporaries in the Western world. During the preceding year and a half he also managed to make his name known in both world and Swedish politics, although he was not yet the controversial figure he was to become later on. Above all, in possession of what he deemed to be sufficient funds, he was eager to return to Asia.

On all of his previous trips to Asia Hedin had traveled across Russia, partly because Russia's possessions in Central Asia were adjacent to the heart of Inner Asia and partly because he could travel within a short distance of that goal by the fast and convenient means of the Russian railroad system. But in the fall of 1905 Russia was in turmoil. The regime of the tsar was under attack, and conditions were not favorable for the foreign traveler. Instead, Hedin traveled as far as Constantinople via Germany and Austria-Hungary and there embarked on a steamer, bound for the Russian port of Batumi on the Black Sea.

Hedin's plan, more ambitious than his earlier ones, was to enter Tibet from British India and to explore the western and central parts of that little-known and isolated land. Since he planned to approach Tibet from the southern, Indian side of the Himalayas, he decided to make his way to India by crossing Persia once more. Specifically, he intended to travel across the northern part of Persia and map that area on the way, particularly the great salt desert called Kavir.

After some difficulties in Russian territory, which was torn by a general strike, Hedin crossed into Persia, organized a caravan of camels in Tehran, and hired five Persian servants. The Persian government provided him with two cavalrymen from the crack corps of cossacks trained by Russian officers, and on January 1, 1906, he left Tehran, bound for the Indian-Persian frontier some 2,400 kilometers to the east.

The journey took four-and-a-half months. Hedin described it in complete detail: the two-volume English translation of his book *Overland to India* is 773 pages long. Journeys across a desert landscape tend to be monotonous, and Hedin's account, which is interrupted and enlivened only by stops in towns and villages and a few descriptive passages, faithfully mirrors that monotony.

Hedin was always fascinated by the desert and attracted to its people and to the ever-present beast of burden of the desert, the camel. The following passage describes nightfall in the desert.

> Soon the last gleam of light dies away in the west, the curtain falls, night builds up its thick walls around us, perspective and distance vanish, the far-distant horizon which lately presented the illusion of a sea has been swallowed up in darkness, and the outlines of the camels are thin and indefinite. . . . But still the air around them is filled with the same never-ending clang of bells, which follows them through the desert; a sonorous, vibrating, ever-repeated and prolonged peal, melting together into a full ringing tone in my ears, a jubilant chord rising up to the sphere of the clouds and stars, spreading its undulations over the surface of the desert; a glorious melody of caravans and wanderers; the triumphal march of the camels, celebrating the victory of their patience over the long distances of the desert in rhythmic waves of song; a hymn as sublimely uniform as the ceaseless, unwearied march of the majestic animals through the dreary wastes of ancient Iran. (1910, 1:365–66)

The great salt desert, the Kavir, inspired Hedin to write of

the lifeless solemnity of the desert, surrounding us on all sides . . . to the south the white sheet of salt has a delusive resemblance to a frozen lake, where the camel skeletons are conspicuous as black specks owing to the dust and dirt which gathers on and about them. (1910, 1:353–54)

There are a few lyrical passages such as these in the two thick volumes of *Overland to India,* but most of the book is a description of a dreary, prolonged journey across an empty landscape. There are numerous photographs of strings of camels against a background of sand and distant mountains, and there are sketches of people encountered in the oases. By today's standards, *Overland to India* has little to offer a reader, but to the public of the first decades of the twentieth century the book was appealing as a description of distant and little-known places, and in that respect Hedin's prose compares well with contemporary works.

On his arrival in India, Hedin wrote a brief report on his journey across Persia to the Royal Geographical Society in London.

My plan was to cross Persia in two months, and I have been three and a half months on my road from Teheran. Now I have the feeling that I have left behind me years of work in the Persian deserts. Among the results of my voyage are two hundred specimens of rocks, fossils from two places, 68 panoramas, 162 sheets of maps, over 100 portraits of natives, and between 400 and 500 photographs. (*Geographical Journal* 13 [1906]:618)

The results of the cartographic work Hedin carried out in his traverse of Persia appeared in 1918 and 1927 in two massive volumes in German. They totaled 687 pages in large format and were illustrated with photographs, watercolor panoramas, and maps. The maps were compiled in Sweden from Hedin's sketches and summarized in eight sheets that were printed as a third, separate volume.

As he described it, Hedin's method for field mapping was identical with the one he had employed more than a decade earlier in the Tarim Basin: he used the pace of his riding camel to measure distance and a compass and watch to estimate direction. Except for when he crossed parts of the salt desert, he followed routes already mapped by others, notably Stahl, the one-time director general of the Persian postal system, and Sykes, a British soldier and diplomat.

The most valuable part of this large work, which was entitled *A Route Survey across Eastern Persia,* is the gazetteer of Persian place names, giving their meaning in German. It was compiled by a Swedish orientalist.

Hedin arrived at the westernmost station of the Indian railroad system, Nushki, late in April, 1906. By mid-May he reached Simla, in the foothills of the Himalayas, which was the summer capital of British India. He was full of confidence about getting help from the British authorities in India, since the viceroy, Lord Curzon, had expressly pledged such assistance.

Writing to Hedin in July, 1905, Curzon had promised that a native surveyor would accompany him and that he would also have an assistant to take astronomical and meteorological observations. Curzon was not certain whether Hedin would run into opposition from the government of Tibet.

> I cannot say what the attitude of the Tibetan government will be at the time you reach India. But if they continue friendly we will of course endeavour to secure for you the required permits and protection. (July 6, 1905)

Hedin was en route to India when two events occurred that were to change British attitudes toward his plans for an expedition to Tibet. First, there was open conflict over military policy between Curzon and the commander-in-chief of the Indian armed forces, Kitchener; as a result, Curzon resigned his office. Second, the coalition government in England was replaced by a Liberal government, and the latter was firmly opposed to the entry of any foreigner into Tibet from Indian territory. Thus Hedin found that his old friend Curzon had been replaced as viceroy by Lord Minto, who was personally very friendly but had to carry out the London government's orders forbidding Hedin to pursue his original plan and enter Tibet by the easy route, from British-controlled territory. Telegrams were sent to London on Hedin's behalf, but permission was denied. Prospects for the Tibetan expedition that Curzon had referred to as "one more big journey before you settle down" (Letter, November 13, 1904) were dim indeed.

But Hedin never gave up easily. His charm and his way of acquiring friends in high places once more worked to his advantage. He managed to obtain letters of introduction to one of the two great leaders of the Tibetan spiritual hierarchy, the Tashi Lama. At the same time, through Swedish contacts he received a passport from the Chinese government allowing him to travel in westernmost China, in Sinkiang province, where he had worked on two occasions in earlier years. The document made no mention of Tibet, but its very existence was likely to impress Chinese officials.

When Hedin left the British summer capital of Simla, he stated that his goal was Leh, capital of the British-controlled westernmost province of Tibet, Ladakh. Thence he professed to continue northward, into Sinkiang. Once in Leh, he assembled a caravan of considerable size: he engaged the services of twenty-one men and bought or hired eighty-eight horses, thirty mules, and ten yaks, as well as sheep and goats. The latter animals served a dual purpose: were the caravan to run into Tibetan officials, Hedin planned to disguise himself as a shepherd, while at the same time some of the animals were destined to provide food for him and his staff.

Hedin started out from Leh in mid-August, 1906, and for the next several months he was "lost." The British authorities expressly forbade him to enter Tibet, but he managed to slip into the wilds of the Tibetan highlands before that order was received by British representatives in Leh, his point of departure.

For the next six months, through the harsh winter of the highlands, Hedin and his caravan wandered eastward across Tibetan territory. He crossed the great chain of mountains that ran parallel to the Himalayas to the north of that range; he measured the elevations of mountain peaks and passes and the depths of remote, salty lakes; he continued to make maps, draw panoramas, and sketch landscapes and people. Most of the time the little

81

group of men and animals pursued its goal alone, rarely meeting Tibetans. But in early February, 1907, Hedin seemed to run once more into the impenetrable wall erected by Tibetan officials and expected to be turned back westward away from his goal, which was the southern Tibetan city of Shigatse, residence of the Tashi Lama.

But this time his luck held. At the moment when local officials, ordered by the government in the capital, Lhasa, were about to forbid him any further travel into Tibet, a courier arrived with sacks of mail for him from the sacred city of Shigatse. Colonel Dunlop Smith, secretary to the viceroy of India and a close friend of Hedin's, had sent the mail, containing letters, newspapers, books, and supplies, to Shigatse, requesting officials of the Tashi Lama's court to forward it to Hedin. Even Hedin himself believed that his being "found" in the wilds of Tibet was a minor miracle. The effect on his Tibetan adversaries was immediate. He was allowed to proceed without further hindrance to the Tashi Lama's residence and was even permitted to make part of the journey by riverboat, on the upper course of the Brahmaputra River.

Hedin managed by careful maneuvers to stay in the holy city for six weeks. His Chinese passport impressed the local Chinese officials (China was the nominal sovereign of Tibet); he was received in friendly fashion by the Tibetan authorities and managed to have an audience with the Tashi Lama, too.

His arrival in Shigatse coincided with the Tibetan New Year, a time of special celebrations, and he was able to photograph and sketch the spectacular ceremonies in Labrang Palace, residence of the Tashi Lama, in complete freedom. The pages of his book on this voyage that describe his stay in Shigatse are a unique and colorful panorama of Tibetan life, including its everyday aspects—marketplaces, horse races, burials—and the religious events that took place during his stay.

During Hedin's sojourn in the holy city of Shigatse, negotiations went on between Lhasa, Peking, and London regarding his future movements, since under the Chinese-British convention of 1904 (established following the British invasion of Tibet) foreigners were not allowed to enter the country. After complex

Sven Hedin, February 10, 1886

Sven Hedin, 1893

Hedin and his parents on his return to Stockholm,
January 17, 1909.

Hedin being greeted by students on his return to Stockholm, January 17, 1909

Farmers' March, February 6, 1914

King Gustav V speaking to Swedish farmers in the courtyard of the royal palace, Stockholm, February 6, 1914

Cartoon by Einar Nerman, Stockholm, 1910. (From *Comedians, Musicians, and Other Folk.*)

Cartoon, 1907. Newspapers: articles on what Sven Hedin is saying.

Cartoon by G. Ljunggren, October 10, 1914. The Kaiser: The courtesy of you, gentlemen, pleases and flatters us a lot — but will you permit a question, how is this possible, isn't Sweden neutral?

King for a day. Mr. Sven Hedin's speech in the palace
courtyard, 1914

Cartoon, *Veckojournalen*, 1915

At home in Stockholm, 1931. *Left to right:* Alma, Clara, Sven, and Emma Hedin.

Sven Hedin, Mongolia, 1936. (Photograph by D. Hummel.)

Sven Hedin, age 80, June 15, 1945

exchanges of letters, Hedin finally was allowed to return to Leh, his point of departure, and on March 27 he and his caravan left Shigatse, bound once more for western Tibet. But it was another seventeen months before he returned to India.

Hedin set two main goals for this expedition: the mapping and surveying of the great mountain chain north of the Himalayas that later he was to call Transhimalaya; and the precise definition of the sources of the great rivers Brahmaputra, Indus, and Sutlej. These he accomplished and thus made a significant contribution to our knowledge of the geography of Tibet.

Hedin published the results of the voyage in a massive work destined for the general public, *Transhimalaya*. Its three volumes (in the English edition) total some 1,300 pages and are profusely illustrated by photographs and sketches made by the author. The narrative is detailed, and like the barren, empty spaces of the Tibetan highlands, tends to be monotonous. But it is enlivened by descriptions of the events that Hedin regarded as high points of his journey; his prose in those passages carries with it the author's enthusiasm about his discoveries.

Other travelers who visited western Tibet before Hedin had established the areas where the sources of the Indus, Brahmaputra, and Sutlej rivers were located. But it fell to Hedin to pinpoint the sources with topographic accuracy, and after carefully measuring water volume and elevation, he stated that what he had described were indeed the sources of these mighty rivers. Thus he was able to define the source of the Brahmaputra, at 4,834 meters above sea level, where a small rivulet issues from a large glacier. In a similar way, he defined the source of the Sutlej, one of the principal rivers of Pakistan, at the point where it leaves the Ganglung Glacier in western Tibet.

Equally important was Hedin's statement that many years after British and Indian surveyors had described the general area of the source of the Indus River, he was able to identify a group of springs that created the actual headwaters of the Indus.

Hedin's other major contribution to the geography of Tibet was his series of measurements, maps, and panoramas describing the Transhimalaya, the great mountain system that runs parallel to the Himalayas, north of the trench occupied by the upper course of the Indus and Brahmaputra. He pointed out in his first popular report that he had made the first recorded crossing of seven of the major passes across the Transhimalaya and had managed to establish the extent, height, and boundaries of that mighty mountain range.

Curzon, an authority on the geography of Inner Asia, wrote that Hedin was the first to establish the existence of the mighty mountain paradise

> tracing for hundreds of miles and the assurance of a definite orographic existence to the mighty mountain palisade or series of palisades to which he has, in my opinion very appropriately, given the title of the Trans-Himalaya. This range has been surmised to exist in its entire length for many years; it has been crossed at the extremities by Littledale and by native surveyors. But it was reserved for Dr. Hedin to trace it on the spot and to place it on the map in its long unbroken, and massive significance. (Curzon 1909, 435–36)

Among the descriptions of the land and the people of Tibet that Hedin offers in *Transhimalaya,* one of the most striking is the passage on the pilgrims circling the holy mountain of Tibet, Mount Kailas. Mount Kailas rises some 6,096 meters above sea level, and around its snowy peak there exists a path 45 kilometers long, followed by the pilgrims making a circuit of the mountain. The Tibetan name for Mount Kailas is Kang-rinpoche, the Holy Ice Mountain. Hedin walked with the pilgrims as they marched

> with light elastic step; they feel neither the icy cold wind nor the scorching sun; every step is a link in a chain which cannot be broken by the powers of evil. . . . During the whole peregrination they pray "Om mani padme hum" (Oh jewel of the lotus flower, amen!) and every time this prayer is uttered they let a bead of the rosary pass through their fingers. (1909–13, 2:197–98)

By April, 1908, Hedin felt satisfied, having accomplished his goal of exploring the Transhimalaya and establishing the exact sources of the Indus, Brahmaputra, and Sutlej. It was at that time the Tibetan authorities decided that they could no longer accept the presence of a wandering European in their land and stopped his caravan. Hedin convinced the Tibetan officials that he was indeed ready to leave the country, and having made another detour rather than following the shortest route, mapping and sketching along the way, he entered India and in mid-September reached Simla.

His stay in Tibet had lasted twenty-eight months. More than once he was considered lost, yet he returned with a rich harvest of observations, maps, photographs, drawings, and paintings, and he was received with open arms by his friends in the British summer capital of India. He was a guest both at the residence of the viceroy and at the house of Lord Kitchener, commander-in-chief of the Indian Army, and shortly after his arrival he presented a formal lecture on his travels to the viceroy and vicereine, Lord and Lady Minto, and their distinguished guests.

Hedin left Simla in October, 1908. The shortest way home would have been by steamer from India to Europe, but ever conscious of the value of public recognition to his future projects, he chose the long route. Responding to an invitation from Japan, he spent a month there, speaking every day at scientific meetings, luncheons, and dinners. He was honored—like his hero Nordenskiöld—by being received by the emperor of Japan and having the gold medal of the Geographical Society of Japan presented to him.

He made his way from Japan through Korea, Manchuria, and Siberia, traveling by railroad. In Moscow his sister Alma met him, and on January 17, 1909, he landed in Stockholm.

Hedin considered the reception extended to him by his countrymen as only slightly more reserved than the one Nordenskiöld had met almost forty years earlier. Thousands of young people filled the waterfront of Stockholm's inner harbor, members of the government and the highest dignitaries of the city and the region welcomed him back home, and he was driven in a carriage of the royal household to the royal palace. There King Gustav V, the royal family, the prime minister, and members of the government met him, and the king, in his welcoming speech, congratulated him on the great and illustrious results of his work in the service of science: "Through your energy and your hard work you have made Sweden's name respected in the world" (1950, 2:12). Then the king presented him the Grand Cross of the North Star, one of the highest Swedish decorations.

A dream had come true for Hedin, the dream he had had when, almost forty years earlier, he had watched Adolf Nordenskiöld land in Stockholm and be acclaimed by his fellow Swedes. Hedin was the man of the hour at home and across Europe. He spoke in London before the Royal Geographical Society and was awarded honorary doctorates by both Oxford and Cambridge. The Berlin Geographical Society honored him with its highest distinction, the Humboldt Medal.

During the summer of 1909 he completed the first two volumes of his report on the expedition, *Transhimalaya,* in record time, something less than four months. He was getting ready to start compiling the scientific results of the expedition, a major undertaking that was not finished until 1922. In the meantime he wrote a two-volume work on world geography for young people, *From Pole to Pole,* that became a best-seller in its original Swedish version in Scandinavia and in German translation throughout Central Europe. It was a well-illustrated introduction to world geography, dealing with all five continents. It was also more proof of Hedin's phenomenal skill at writing, this time in popular style. It made his name a household word and contributed a substantial sum in royalties to his coffers, which had been depleted by the expenses of his Asian travels.

Tireless traveler, prolific writer, the best-known man in Sweden at the time, Sven Hedin managed to keep in touch with what was happening in his homeland and in world affairs. The time between his return from Asia in 1909 and the outbreak of the First World War in 1914 was one of continuing tension in Europe, and Hedin soon became deeply involved in Swedish politics.

X

Politician and War Correspondent, 1911–18

During the years immediately preceding the First World War, Sweden was deeply divided on issues of foreign policy. The conservatives remembered Sweden's "Time of Greatness," the seventeenth and early eighteenth centuries, when Swedish armies won victories on German, Russian, and Polish soil, and Sweden was the leading power of Northern Europe. They were in favor of increasing Sweden's military strength and lengthening the time of compulsory military service.

The supporters of the center and left in Sweden remembered the price the country had had to pay when the Time of Greatness ended in defeat and the long and expensive military adventures left the country destitute. That poverty, in their view, was responsible for the great wave of emigration from Sweden to the New World during the nineteenth century; it was not until wide-ranging social and economic reforms were introduced in the late 1800s that emigration slowed down. The center and left parties wanted to preserve those reforms; they were reluctant to increase the burden of armaments and opposed what they considered military posturing.

Sven Hedin was first and foremost a Swedish patriot, but he always had a special place for Germany in his heart and from his student days in Berlin to the end of his life remained a faithful supporter of all things German. His views of European affairs never changed: Germany was Sweden's best friend and most likely ally, and Russia was Sweden's traditional enemy. Conservative by temperament, proud of Sweden's past glories, and dedicated to a close relationship between Sweden and Germany, Hedin stood squarely with the conservative right in Swedish politics.

The issue of a new heavy cruiser to be built for the Swedish

Navy became the rallying point for the conservatives: in 1910, a bill to build such a vessel was introduced in Parliament, but the following year's elections brought a center-left coalition to power, and the new government decided to postpone the building of the new warship. The conservatives, supported by the military and by the royal court, wanted to alert public opinion to the need for rearmament and looked for the best way to make their views known. They decided to ask Hedin to speak for them: he was the best-known Swede of the time; he was a patriot; he considered Russia Sweden's traditional enemy; and he strongly believed in a rapprochement between Sweden and Germany. He had been a spokesman for Sweden at the time of the Swedish-Norwegian crisis; surely he would make himself available again.

A small group of army officers was dedicated to the notion of putting the point of view of the armed forces before the Swedish public, and one of their number, Major Gabriel Hedengren, called on Hedin in December, 1911. Hedengren explained that since public concern over national defense was too weak to influence the politicians, the time was right for direct action. He proposed that Hedin should organize a lecture tour across Sweden and support rearmament in his lectures. Hedin was prepared to act for a cause he fully believed in, but doubted that a lecture tour would have much effect, since only a small number of people would attend. Instead, he suggested to Hedengren that a short pamphlet on the issue of national defense should be prepared, to be printed in a large number of copies and distributed, free, to all the households in the country, as a supplement to daily newspapers that supported the conservative point of view. Hedengren would provide facts on national defense, Hedin would supply his own worldview.

The military group around Hedengren managed to get financial support, and in January, 1912, a slim pamphlet entitled "A Word of Warning" was distributed across Sweden. One million copies were printed. Its opening sentence set the tone: "Like a heavy, darkening fog in the dark days of autumn, awareness of an insidious worry is spreading over Sweden."

Russia and Sweden had been antagonists for a long time,

Hedin reminded his readers, and Russia had been the winner the last time the two countries went to war, in 1809. Russia overran and annexed Finland at that time and managed to carry the war onto Swedish soil.

> In 1809 we lost Finland. In 1905 we lost Norway. Now it is Sweden's turn. It concerns our people, our freedom, our very existence. It concerns our country, our dear old Sweden, our farms and our fields, our roads, our villages, our cities. (1912, 7)

Russia was Sweden's most dangerous opponent, in Hedin's view, and its desire for an ice-free port was a direct menace. Since the Russian drive to the Pacific had been thwarted by Japan, Russia's next and logical move would be to open a corridor across northernmost Sweden and Norway to the Atlantic Ocean; Norway, independent since 1905, would be too weak to resist.

What chance would Sweden have to oppose the advance of Russia, the greatest military power in Europe, Hedin asked. In his view, Sweden's defeat was a foregone conclusion. After painting a dark and dismal picture of Sweden under enemy occupation, Hedin came to the main point of the pamphlet, the strengthening of the country's defenses, including longer compulsory military service. After all, Hedin wrote, he had had to live for long months under extremely difficult conditions in the wilds of Asia; Swedish youth could and should endure hardships in the defense of their country. There should not be any debate on national defense, no controversy on that issue at all; in his view it was a matter of survival.

"A Word of Warning" was read by most Swedes. Overnight, Sven Hedin became the standard bearer of the conservatives and the principal spokesman for rearmament. His newly acquired fame as a political figure was soon strengthened by several speeches on national defense that he made in 1913. The occasion was a grand tour of Sweden that Hedin undertook that year in order to get to know his own country as well as Inner Asia, as he put it at the time.

Hedin's grand tour was prompted by his election to the Swedish Academy, a distinguished body created in the late 1700s by King Gustav III on the model of the French Academy. Like its French counterpart, the Swedish Academy was entrusted with the task of guarding the country's language and ideals. Because it quickly became a symbol of the highest standards in literature, Alfred Nobel selected it as the organization to award the Nobel Prize for literature. Membership was a very high honor; it also demanded that each newly elected member honor his predecessor with a formal address on the occasion of his taking the seat of that deceased member. Hedin was elected to replace the head of Sweden's Archaeological Survey, and in order to prepare his address he decided to visit a number of the sites where his predecessor had conducted archaeological work. It was during his travels across Sweden in 1913 that Hedin spoke out on the issue of rearmament.

The most important speech he made was at an officers' mess in the mining city of Falun. Hedin was a dinner guest of the general manager of the Falun copper mine, and among those present at the dinner was the commanding officer of the regiment quartered in Falun, Colonel Björkman. After dinner, the colonel invited Hedin to the regiment's officers' mess for coffee. In keeping with Swedish custom, Hedin was toasted by his host, and custom demanded that he respond. His speech, even though it was made before a private gathering, was published in the Swedish press.

Hedin used strong words to criticize the government's stand on rearmament.

We see the sitting government putting the freedom of our fatherland on a card in a game, and by letting our defenses decay, play heads or tails with our national independence. We ask ourselves, is this the same country that, two hundred years ago, had a young king who saved our land? (1951, 8–14)

Hedin spoke of Charles XII, the warrior king of the eighteenth century, who was at the moment the center of a cult, a national symbol made popular by the writings of the Swedish poet Verner von Heidenstam. But Hedin did not refer to past events. He

Bridge over the Tigris, Bagdad, 1886

Aga Hassan, Kirmanshah, 1886

Khosro, 75 years old, Bokhara, 1890

Turdu Bek, a Kirghiz, Turngart, 1890

Turkmens, Merv, 1890

Pir Mahmud Kara Beg, a Tadzhik,
Darvas, 1890

Yezdikazd village, Iran, 1887

"Some of my servants with our yaks." Mount Muztagh-Ata, at 6,300 meters, 1894

Lop Nor, 1896

Camel, 1906

Dancing lama, Shigatse, 1907

Tsangla Valley, Tibet, 1906

Masked lama, Shigatse, 1907

Sungnak, 72 years old, Shigatse, 1907

Lamasery, Shigatse, 1907

Lamas in a temple courtyard, Shigatse, 1907

Flute player, Shigatse, 1907

Mongol beggar, 1907

New Year's feast, Shigatse, 1907

Drum player, Shigatse, 1907

Pilgrim of Pembo sect, Mount Kailas, Tibet, 1908

An Arab, Damascus, 1916

Ivan Popov, Russian prisoner of war, 1915

openly attacked the sitting government in an officers' mess, among members of the armed forces of Sweden, who were under the control of a civilian government. His speech had a strong impact. Colonel Björkman was court-martialed for allowing Hedin to use such language in front of a group of officers, but he was acquitted of the charge of insubordination. As for Hedin, his credentials as a representative of the right were strengthened, and he became the spokesman for Swedish rearmament.

A few weeks after the Falun incident, on October 5, 1913, Hedin spoke out again, before a group of young people from Dalarna, a district north of Stockholm. He reminded his listeners that while their elected government was the only one in Europe to reduce armaments in a time of grave international tension, the Swedish people had made their views known by raising, through public subscription, a sum large enough to build the new warship whose construction was being indefinitely postponed by the government in office.

Hedin went on to say:

> I have no interests here in Sweden, I do not own a single brick of a building. I can travel in Asia, no matter what flag is flown from the royal palace in Stockholm. I can write books as easily in London or in Berlin as here at home. But my roots are deep in Sweden, in the district of Närke, where my ancestors were farmers and preachers in our Time of Greatness. Therefore I consider it the greatest disaster, the most humiliating shame that could strike our people, if our fortresses were to surrender, our army lay down its arms before the conqueror's army, if our land were to become a province in the victor's empire, and our ancient freedom exchanged for slavery. (1951, 105–8)

The government of Sweden had become a target for its opponents both in and out of Parliament. Hedin by this time was so committed to the cause of rearmament that he composed a second pamphlet, "A Second Word of Warning," like its predecessor printed in hundreds of thousands of copies. This time he viewed the future in an even darker light: "Listen, ye Swedes! What are the church bells ringing for? Is it a funeral, is it a thousand-year old country being carried to the grave?" (1913, 1). In Hedin's mind, the choice was clear-cut. It was a time to decide between the forces of good and evil.

By late fall, 1913, the conflict between the Swedish government, representing the elected majority in Parliament, and the forces demanding rearmament of the country was approaching a crisis. Sweden was a constitutional monarchy, and the powers of the Crown were limited by the constitution. But the court did not view the government in office with favor, and those close to King Gustav V urged him to assume a stronger role in running the country. Queen Victoria was particularly insistent: she was a German by birth, first cousin to Emperor William II of Germany, and eager to see her husband play as important a part in government as William II.

Two groups were particularly insistent on direct action by the king, hoping he would openly oppose the government on the issue of national defense and thus bring about its downfall. One was a group of army officers who were in favor of the king's taking over command of the armed forces; it submitted to the Crown a secret memorandum urging action along those lines. At the same time another group, influential businessmen and landowners, decided that the best way to get direct action was to organize a large demonstration in Stockholm in support of the king, thus spurring him to speak out more openly on defense matters.

Both groups chose Hedin as their spokesman. He was visited by Lieutenant Carl Bennedich, representing the group of army officers, and by Uno Nyberg and Jarl Frykberg, representing the civilian group planning the mass demonstration in Stockholm. Hedin agreed to work with the two groups, and by the end of 1913 preparations were well under way for what became known as the "Farmers' March." After consultations with the court, the event was scheduled for February 6, 1914, in Stockholm, and the organizers set out to recruit the greatest possible number of participants for a demonstration of loyalty to the Crown. In the meantime, Hedin and Lieutenant Bennedich drafted a speech that they hoped the king would deliver on the occasion. Their draft was completed on January 24, and on the following day Hedin was received by the king.

For many years Hedin had been a special favorite of the Swedish court, ennobled by King Oscar II and honored again by King Oscar's son, Gustav V. King Gustav knew the purpose of the audience he granted to Hedin, and after reading the draft of the speech he declared, "I shall make this speech to the farmers on February 6. Nothing will be added to it or changed. It has everything I will say" (1951, 302).

On February 5, 1914, over 30,000 men came to Stockholm. They spent the night in barracks, in schools, in churches, in private homes. The next morning they marched to the royal palace, arranged in groups carrying placards that bore the names of their home districts. They were met in the courtyard by King Gustav V and members of the royal family.

After the leader of the march presented an address of loyalty and support, King Gustav spoke to the assembly. He recalled the strong, traditional bonds that had always existed between the rulers and the people of Sweden and added that "no other king who wore Sweden's crown had had the privilege to stand face to face with the common folk of Sweden and listen to their voice" (Manuscript, Hedin family collection). The king called for strengthening the nation's defenses and for longer military service for conscripts, and he pledged his full support for these measures.

The speech to the Farmers' March was an open challenge to the government in office: Staaff, the prime minister, who did not know about the speech before it was delivered, called on the king and asked for his assurance that in the future the government would be informed of the monarch's political speeches in advance. King Gustav refused the request, saying that he would not give up his right to speak freely to the Swedish people. It was a clash between two interpretations of the constitution, and on February 10, Staaff's government resigned. The king asked the conservatives to form a new government, and that government was the one that led Sweden through the years of the First World War.

Hedin, honored as an explorer and scientist and acclaimed as a political activist, now had the added satisfaction of being a speech-writer for the king of Sweden. Some time later, in 1915, he wrote to Major Hedengren, who had worked with him on the manuscript of "A Word of Warning":

> It was really "A Word of Warning" that started it! All that came afterwards was but an echo. It was "A Word of Warning" that awakened our people, and I shall remember as long as I live the days and nights we worked together in my study. We can look back on that time with pleasure. We were there first! We can be pleased with the blow we struck then. (January 30, 1915)

Sweden's conservative government believed in strong national defense, but it continued to be neutral. In May, 1914, Prime Minister Hammarskjöld, a conservative, responded to a question in Parliament regarding a speech Hedin had made in Oslo calling for a Swedish-German alliance. Rearmament, Hammarskjöld said, was only undertaken to defend Swedish neutrality (Gihl 1968, 280–83).

Three months after this reaffirmation of Swedish neutrality, Europe was at war. Germany, the strongest of the so-called Central Powers, was almost immediately accused of disregarding the accepted rules for the conduct of war and committing atrocities against civilians in German-occupied areas. Hedin felt that as a citizen of a neutral country he would be well qualified to write an objective report on Germany at war, and he offered his services to the German government. Germany was delighted to have a close friend inspect its conduct of the war, and on September 11, 1914, Hedin left Stockholm to tour the western front.

He spent two months in Belgium and France, was a guest of William II at imperial headquarters in Luxemburg, met German royalty and the commanders of German land and sea forces, and within two months of his return to Sweden published a detailed report in two volumes totaling 800 pages: *From the Western Front*. It was a well-written work, fully sympathetic to the German cause, and a big success in its German version. Published in Germany under the title *Ein Volk in Waffen* (A people in arms), it was distributed to German troops in hundreds of thousands of copies.

Encouraged by the success of his first venture as a war correspondent, Hedin returned to Germany in February, 1915, this time by invitation from the chief of the German General Staff, Field Marshal von Moltke. The German military attaché in Stockholm issued a special passport for the occasion, bearing this identification: "for Dr. Sven Hedin, the true friend of Germany."

The journey in the spring and summer of 1915 took Hedin to the Russian front. On his return, he prepared another extensive report, 900 printed pages long, entitled *War against Russia: Memories from the Eastern Front, March—August, 1915*. The German translation, more martial in its title, *Nach Osten!* (To the East!), was again a big success, both in Germany and in Austria-Hungary. But reaction from the Allies was different. Hedin was attacked as a German propagandist, and several English and French scientific organizations withdrew the honors they had bestowed on him earlier.

None of that mattered much to Hedin. Germany, the country he admired, was winning the war, and he was, he believed, presenting objective reports on the German war effort. In fact, Hedin's books portrayed Emperor William II and his generals and admirals as supermen, and in his mind German victory was a foregone conclusion. He defended any and all German deeds and policies, to the extent of defending Turkey, Germany's ally, against the accusation of having massacred hundreds of thousands of Armenians. The Armenian massacres were really a figment of the imagination of English propagandists, wrote Hedin; the fate of the Armenians was brought upon them by their disloyalty to the Turkish state (1918, 64–65).

As he had always done on his travels, Hedin recorded his observations in notes, photographs, and drawings. But his drawings are far less partisan than his published writings; he saw and he showed the sufferings of men and women, of Russians and Englishmen, of Germans, Austrians, and Turks, in the turmoil of war.

Having covered, in 1914 and 1915, the two principal fighting fronts where German armies were in action, Hedin next turned to the war in the Middle East. Once more he wanted to return to Asia. Permission was granted, and in 1916 Hedin traveled for seven months throughout the Middle East, visiting Syria, Palestine, Mesopotamia, and Lebanon. This time he viewed everything more as a tourist than a war correspondent; the closest he got to any military action was during his visit to the Suez Canal.

The two books that resulted from this journey, *Bagdad, Babylon, Niniveh* and *To Jerusalem,* were first published in Sweden in 1917 and soon thereafter in German translation. Once more, Hedin managed to write vividly about his travels, illustrating the books with photographs of civilians and fighting men and with some of his finest pencil portraits of people. The time he spent at home was devoted to work on the scientific results of his last journey to Tibet, but his main concern was the progress of the war.

Writing to his German publisher and close friend, Brockhaus, in April, 1918, when the last major German offensive was in progress on the western front, he told Brockhaus that the French government had stripped him of the honors it had granted him before the war and had asked that he return diplomas and insignia of the Legion of Honor to the French Minister in Stockholm. "It is marvelous that they think of such bagatelles on the threshold of their annihilation. They will not achieve victory with such means" (1942, 287).

As late as June, 1918, Hedin still believed Germany would win the war. "I look forward with excitement and longing to the great victory; I have no doubts about the outcome," he wrote Brockhaus (1942, 290). But the end was only a few months away. In early October, 1918, Hedin was visiting Berlin and attending a session of the German Parliament when the newly appointed German chancellor accepted the American proposals for ending the war, President Wilson's Fourteen Points (Essén 1959, 134). Another month went by, and on November 11, 1918, Germany surrendered.

The same day, in an article published in a Stockholm newspaper, Hedin wrote:

Democracy cannot tolerate strong and manly personalities. Kaiser Wilhelm is the last, the only true ruling personality of our time. . . . He knew that he was the most important man of our generation and, until recently, the most powerful. It is because of that he is considered an obstacle to mediocrity. (November 11, 1918)

XI

Writer, Scientist, Lecturer, World Traveler, 1918–26

For five years, from 1913 through 1918, Hedin devoted most of his time to political causes; he was involved in the conflict between liberals and conservatives at home, and he reported the German war effort abroad. The books and pamphlets that resulted from his work as a war correspondent total thousands of pages, and it would be reasonable to assume that he would have had no time left to devote to other writings. Yet these were the years when he produced some of the best and most important works of his long career and wrote his most successful popular book, *From Pole to Pole*, and his most important scientific contribution, the massive volumes of *Southern Tibet*.

From Pole to Pole was first published in Sweden in 1911 and appeared in many editions, both in its original version and German translation, during the next quarter of a century. It was also translated and published in eleven other languages besides Swedish and German. A well-written introduction to the wonders of the world, it was as much a part of the lives of children growing up in Scandinavia and Central Europe during the 1920s and 1930s as their schoolbooks were. It was Hedin's most successful and most lucrative venture in popular writing.

The nine volumes of *Southern Tibet: Discoveries in Former Times Compared with My Own Researches, 1906–1908* were published between 1917 and 1922. Their format was large, their illustrative material lavishly produced, their scholarship impeccable. These volumes represent Hedin's most significant contribution to geography. Although he secured the cooperation of specialists in geology, botany, meteorology, and Chinese history, Hedin himself coordinated their efforts and wrote the bulk of the published material.

Southern Tibet deals with a much larger area than its title suggests. It is in fact a complete survey of the physical geography of a large part of Central Asia. It recounts the long process by which that remote and forbidding land was unveiled, and it deals with the past as well as the present. Hedin describes the exploration and mapping of Tibet from the beginning centuries of the Christian era to the early years of the twentieth century. He evaluates geographers' descriptions and explorers' reports and legends and reproduces in facsimile the most important maps of the region made from the late fifteenth to the early twentieth century. The result is a milestone in geographical research, the most important work on the physical geography of Tibet ever printed.

Southern Tibet overwhelms the reader by its sheer size: the eight volumes of text together with the separate index volume total 3,547 pages. Hedin was responsible for much of the material, 2,343 printed pages. In addition to the text there are two portfolios containing ninety-eight maps compiled from Hedin's own sketch maps drawn in the field and an album with 552 panoramas, also drawn by him.

Hedin dedicated the work to the Survey of India, one of the world's leading mapping agencies.

> The survey of the whole of the Himalayas and Western Karakoram is a most brilliant work, and no official survey of any state in the world can be compared with it, none has had greater difficulties to overcome. . . . As it is, the work of the Survey is gigantic and admirable. (1917–22, 7:457–58)

The first volume of Hedin's work deals with the area surrounding Lake Manasarowar in southwest Tibet and with the sources of the great Indian rivers, the Indus, the Sutlej, and the Tsangpo-Brahmaputra. It also describes the efforts of early explorers. In its own way, this and the other historical portions of *Southern Tibet* appear to have fulfilled Hedin's ambition to produce a work that would compare with those of his hero, Adolf Nordenskiöld. Nordenskiöld dealt with the history of mapmaking in general, and Hedin focused on the history of the exploration and mapping of Tibet and adjacent parts of Central Asia. The detailed, eminently readable, and admirably illustrated historical survey contained in the first volume of the work is followed, in the second volume, by a brief description of Hedin's own travels in the region and of his discovery of the sources of the great Indian rivers.

In the first part of volume 3, Hedin once more reports in considerable detail on earlier exploration and mapping of the mighty mountain system north of the Himalayas that he had named Transhimalaya. In the second part, he follows this with a presentation of his own crossings of the Transhimalaya, relying on his drawings as much as his words.

> For thoroughly penetrating my description of the topography and morphology of Tibet, it is necessary to "read" my atlas of panoramas as if it were a book. The only difference is that the words and lines in a book are in this atlas changed into mountain ranges and summits, . . . (1917–22, 4:28–29)

Hedin considers of the greatest importance the fact that much of the Transhimalaya system was never fully known before his own journeys.

> As to the Central Transhimalaya, it was absolutely unknown. A part of it had been skirted by Nain Sing in the north, its southern flank had been followed by Ryder's and Rawling's memorable expedition. Between these two routes the *terra incognita* was situated, and I went out to fill up the blanks, so far as my forces allowed. (1917–22, 3:225)

The name Transhimalaya was first suggested some thirty years before Hedin's expedition by one of the chiefs of the Survey of India, Godwin-Austen, but it was Hedin who spent much of his time and energy in getting the scientific world to accept it. Yet the only major atlas now in use that employs the term Transhimalaya, rather than a set of local names, for parts of the system is the *Great Soviet World Atlas,* published in the mid-1950s.

Volume 4 of *Southern Tibet* describes Hedin's own travels in the western part of the country, a subject he had presented earlier to the general public in his book *Transhimalaya*. But this time the report is more factual, stripped of personal observations and the descriptions of people as well as places that had enlivened the earlier, popular work. Instead, Hedin presents detailed data on each of the 482 camps, or stops, on his journey, giving the altitude of each and the difference in altitude and the distance in kilometers between them. The work becomes truly impressive when one takes into account not only the physical effort required to travel (more often than not by foot) long distances across difficult terrain that was always at altitudes above 4,000 meters, but also the effort and determination involved in taking meteorological and geological as well as astronomical observations, reading instruments, keeping a detailed journal, photographing, and drawing hundreds of sketch maps, views, and panoramas.

Volume 7 is the last volume in the set that includes Hedin's own material based on his travels. This volume is, first, an account of the history of the exploration of the Karakoram Mountains from ancient times to the twentieth century. It includes a graphic history of the subject and a series of maps that spans more than four centuries. Equally important, this volume also contains Hedin's own summary of his views on the physical geography of Tibet, which in many details still prevail.

Volume 6 of *Southern Tibet* is made up of contributions by subject specialists on aspects of the physical geography of much of Tibet, based on data recorded during Hedin's journeys. Anders Hennig describes and analyzes nearly 1,200 rock samples and establishes a geological and petrographical classification for them. On the basis of these samples, Hennig presents generalized geological notions on the structure of Tibet, illustrated by fifteen geological profiles.

Nils Ekholm presents an analysis of the meteorological observations Hedin made, which included the longitude and latitude of each station and its elevation, air pressure, temperature in degrees Celsius, humidity, readings of solar radiation, wind speed and direction, cloud cover, and precipitation.

K. G. Olsson tabulates the astronomical observations collected by Hedin in ninety-six series of data. These are of particular value since they were taken in numerous locations in the Tibetan highlands where such data had never been available before. In the final section of this volume C. H. Ostenfeld surveys the botanical specimens Hedin had brought back and lists flowering plants, mosses, bacillaries, and algae. These geological, meteorological, astronomical, and botanical materials add greatly to the value of *Southern Tibet* and are an important part of the literature of these subjects.

Volume 8 differs from the others, being essentially a series of studies of materials relating to China. The first segment, written jointly by Hedin and by the German China specialist Albert Herrmann, is a historical survey of Chinese knowledge of the Ts'ungling Mountains of western China. It is followed by a major essay of over 300 pages, written by Herrmann, on the history of Chinese mapmaking, specifically on the way in which the Chinese depicted their knowledge of countries to the west of China. This treatise remains an indispensable guide to the subject, a treasure house of information that lists, analyzes, and in many cases reproduces important Chinese maps dating from the first millenium B.C. to the late nineteenth century. The volume also includes a short essay on two Chinese manuscript maps of western China that are of Turki origin and a list of Chinese forms of place names on old maps.

The final volume of the series, volume 9, is introduced by Hedin's brief report on his explorations in the Eastern Pamirs in 1894–95. This is followed by a glossary of place names in Sinkiang province that are of Turki origin, a short essay on the geology of the Eastern Pamirs by the Swedish geologist Bror Asklund, and two contributions describing old Chinese reports on Tibet and the Chinese-Tibetan borderlands. The index to the entire set of volumes appears at the end of volume 9; it includes lists of persons, places, and subjects. The index was referred to, in a review of the entire work, as "an admirable tool, henceforth indispensable for all research on the geography of Asia, truly a model of its kind" (de Margerie 1929, 129).

Southern Tibet appeared between 1916 and 1922. Five volumes, one set of maps, and the atlas of panoramas were published in Stockholm, and four volumes appeared in Leipzig. It is surprising that specialized geographical journals reviewed *Southern Tibet* only in a brief, superficial way, bearing witness to the reviewers' unwillingness to devote enough time to read and analyze a work of such importance. Only the *Times Literary Supplement,* of London, recognized the significance of Hedin's magnum opus. It called the work

> a set of large and learned volumes that carry us a long way forward in our knowledge of the mountains and plains, the rivers and lakes, and the other physical features of the great Tibetan tableland. For our latter-day geographical knowledge of Tibet, we owe more to the author of this work than to any other explorer. (Reviewed July 12, 1923)

It was not until 1928 that a major review that did justice to the scientific importance of *Southern Tibet* appeared. It was published in Paris under the title *The Works of Sven Hedin and the Orography of Tibet,* and the author, Emmanuel de Margerie, a distinguished French geographer, paid tribute to Hedin's work. He calls the *Southern Tibet* series "one of the most sumptuous publications ever dedicated to the study of Asia" and concludes that "this eminent geographer . . . will keep his reputation, rightly earned, as one of the greatest travelers of all time" (de Margerie 1929, 131–32).

But *Southern Tibet* and *From Pole to Pole* do not represent all of Hedin's writings during the crucial years 1916 to 1922. Having already attempted biographical writing in 1891, when he published a book on the Russian explorer Przhevalsky's journeys in Inner Asia, Hedin suggested to the Swedish Academy a book on the life and travels of a Swedish personality of the Renaissance, Bengt Bengsson Oxenstierna. His first essay on Oxenstierna appeared in the academy's official publication series in 1918, and widespread interest in the topic prompted him to enlarge its scope. In 1921 a tome of 544 pages entitled *Bengt the Traveler* appeared in Stockholm.

Bengt Bengtsson Oxenstierna, scion of a Swedish family of considerable distinction, was born in 1591. He studied at the University of Rostock in northern Germany, and between 1612 and 1620, after completing his studies, he traveled widely in Europe and in the Middle East. He served as a diplomat and as governor of Swedish possessions in the Baltic and Swedish-held cities in Germany; he died in 1643. Hedin was fascinated by the fact that Oxenstierna visited places in Persia he himself had first seen in his youth, and he compiled a large volume based on the slender contemporary accounts of his subject's travels, generously padded with excerpts from accounts left behind by Oxenstierna's contemporaries. The resulting volume is really more of an anthology of Renaissance travel and travelers than a true biography.

While working on scientific reports and writing biographical sketches, Hedin also devoted considerable time to a book unique among the many he produced during his long and busy life. Published in two volumes in 1920 and 1922, the work entitled *Tsangpo Lama's Pilgrimage* does not fit any of the several categories of scientific and political literature Hedin had contributed to. His German bibliographer calls it a poem, and it may truly be described as a poem in prose.

The story of Tsangpo Lama is a piece of fiction. It contains some of the most beautiful passages Hedin ever wrote, and it has been suggested that the first part of the story may even be autobiographical. The book deals with a young Mongol chieftain who decides to follow the contemplative life of a Buddhist monk rather than inherit his father's position as chief of his tribe and marry a beautiful Mongol princess. His decision is made when he watches the entry into Peking of the second-highest dignitary of the Lamaist faith, the Tashi Lama, who comes to the Chinese capital to visit the Emperor Ch'ien-lung. The story is set in the late eighteenth century but is really timeless; and the background of most of the action is not Peking nor even the nearby monastery at Jehol, but the wide-open spaces of westernmost China and Tibet.

The Tashi Lama dies during his visit to the emperor's court in Peking, and his body is to be carried back to his residence, the great monastery of Tashi Lunpo in Shigatse, Tibet, for burial. The young Mongol prince, having become a lama himself, participates in the pilgrimage to Tibet, hence the title of the book. *Tsangpo Lama's Pilgrimage* is full of allegories and images taken from Hedin's travels: the hero's name is that of the river Tsangpo, which becomes the Brahmaputra where it enters India, and it was Hedin who located the sources of that great stream.

After entering Tibet, Tsangpo Lama is kidnapped by local marauding tribesmen, and part of the story is that of his adventures among his captors, his escape, and his attempt to rejoin the pilgrim's caravan on its way to the great sanctuary in Tibet. In an essay contributed to the volume honoring Hedin on his seventieth birthday, the German geographer Wegener, a fellow student of Hedin's in Berlin, managed to condense in a few words the spirit of this extraordinary piece of fiction.

> The true hero of this work is not Tsangpo Lama at all, or any other human being in it. The object of the ecstatic, glowing spirit that pervades the book . . . is the land and the life of Inner Asia. It is this strange and powerful world of deserts, steppes, and high mountains that had become the background for Hedin's own life . . . this world of endless horizons, of peaks pointing to the sky, of inspiring solitude, of glittering lakes and glaciers, with its strange, wild, and free life, its frightening storms and silent, starlit nights, its wild beasts and birds, rough hunters and highwaymen, shepherds, monks singing liturgy, its tempting mysteries and frightening dangers. (Wegener 1935, 467)

Tsangpo Lama's Pilgrimage is not a novel. Rather, it is a series of magnificent vignettes of the people, the animals, and the nature of Mongolia and Tibet. Hedin describes a fire on the Gobi desert that forces Mongol herdsmen to round up their precious camels to prevent the destruction of their sole source of wealth; a small band of hermits living out a life of contemplation on an island in an icy lake high in Tibet; and the yearly wanderings of shepherds driving their flocks to market to exchange sheep and the salt they carry for their own needs. His sketches of the animals of Inner

Asia include masterly descriptions of the daily struggle for existence waged by wild asses and yaks and marmots. *Tsangpo Lama's Pilgrimage* contains some of the finest writing and most striking imagery Sven Hedin ever put on paper.

The second volume of *Tsangpo Lama's Pilgrimage* was completed and published in 1922, which also saw the publication of the last part of *Southern Tibet*. During that year, Hedin had given a series of lectures in Germany, partly in response to popular demand and partly to replenish his coffers, which had been seriously depleted by the expensive volumes of *Southern Tibet*. In addition to public and private support, their publication had required Hedin to contribute substantial sums from his own pocket. After seeing the books published and giving the lectures, Hedin took a winter vacation on the Italian Riviera and decided that what he really wanted to do next was travel around the world.

Hedin sailed from Hamburg to New York in February, 1923, for an American lecture tour. His lectures were well attended, he met several leading Americans, among them Henry Ford, and on his way to California he visited the Grand Canyon. To see that great wonder of nature had long been a goal of his, and on his return to Sweden a year later, he published his impressions of it in a short book that was handsomely illustrated with his own watercolors and sketches.

The next leg of the journey took him across the Pacific to Japan and China, on his way to Russia. He followed the route from Peking to southern Siberia that he had taken some twenty years earlier (traveling by car rather than the traditional horse-drawn cart) and took the Trans-Siberian railroad to Moscow. As he put it in the foreword to his book describing the journey from Peking to Moscow, he was interested in the "new Russia," and he described his experiences there rather than discussing the principles and policies of the Bolshevik regime.

The winter of 1923 was an exciting time to be in Russia. When Hedin arrived in Moscow in December, Lenin was still the leader of the country, although he was severely ill and could no longer look after the day-to-day matters of public policy and administration. Hedin was met not only by Swedish friends then in the

Russian capital but also by an official of the Russian foreign office who brought him an invitation to call on the commissar for foreign affairs, Chicherin. That interview was but one of many Hedin had during his stay in Moscow. He was feted by the scientific community of the capital and was wined and dined at numerous public functions.

One of the functions he described in detail was a meeting of the Moscow City Soviet, or city council, then still presided over by one of the "Old Bolsheviks," Kamenev. Hedin was impressed by the high standard of the proceedings at the meeting and thought that Kamenev, a battle-scarred revolutionary, spoke like a university professor rather than an agitator. "The revolutionary days are over, there is no longer any need for fiery speeches," wrote Hedin (1924, 241).

In the book he published on his return to Sweden, *Peking to Moscow,* Hedin called for closer scientific ties with Russia and for Swedish recognition of the Soviet government (1924, 267–68). He also described the highlight of his stay in Moscow: his lecture on Tibet before an audience composed mostly of scientists, at the "House of Scholars." His audience also included two members of the Soviet government: Commissar for Foreign Affairs Chicherin and Commissar for Public Health Semashkin, who introduced Hedin.

Hedin asked the audience if he could speak in German, saying that it had been a long time since he had spoken Russian in public. "Nyet, nyet, pa russkii, pa russkii," they demanded. Hedin then proceeded to give a lengthy presentation on his travels in Tibet. Afterwards, there was a banquet in his honor, and Foreign Affairs Commissar Chicherin formally thanked him. In his answer, reproduced in *Peking to Moscow,* Hedin spoke of his feelings toward Russia and Russians:

I am an admirer of Russian science, Russian literature, Russian art, Russian music. I shall report to my fellow Swedes on what I saw and experienced in Russia. I shall work toward reestablishing relations between Swedish and Russian scientists. Thus, Sweden will become the connecting link between Russian and Western scientists. I am pleased that political storms did not destroy scientific work in Russia. (1924, 310)

Hedin went on to say, "This is the eighteenth time I visited Russia. I am no stranger here, I feel at home in Russia." And he added some remarks on his personal life that were startling in their candor.

It might interest the ladies present why I am not married. I have been in love many times, but Asia remained my bride. She has held me captive in her cold embrace, and out of jealously would never let me love any other. And I have been faithful to her, that is certain. (1924, 311)

On his return to Sweden, Hedin was received in a cold and unfriendly fashion. It was surprising, to say the least, that a conservative would speak of Russia without referring to terror and tyranny. But Hedin stuck to his guns. "Russia is what it is, Sweden should be sympathetic to a peaceful Russia, but should be well armed against Russia that could threaten our borders," he said to a group of Swedish Communists in Stockholm (Wennerholm 1978, 198–99).

XII

The Sino-Swedish Expedition, 1926–35

His world tour over, Hedin once more started planning for yet another journey to Asia. Seeking support for another expedition, Hedin found it this time in Germany. Germany had lost the First World War, but by the mid-1920s it was back once more in the community of nations, ambitious and outward looking. No other foreigner was as respected and popular in Germany as Sven Hedin, and his popularity paved the way toward organizing his next adventure in Asia.

Support for what was to be Hedin's last expedition came from an unexpected source. On August 29, 1925, Admiral Levetzow, a former aide to Emperor William II, and Captain Florman, a former officer of the German Air Force, called on Hedin in Stockholm. They brought a message from Hugo Junkers, one of the world's leading aircraft designers, inviting Hedin to Junkers's headquarters in Dessau, Germany. Junkers wanted to organize a consortium of a dozen or more European countries to control a worldwide airline network. Each country was to have a representative at the organizing conference, and Hedin was to represent Sweden.

Hedin protested, saying that he did not know anything about airplanes or air transport. Admiral Levetzow replied, "Professor Junkers has grandiose plans, to create a worldwide air network, using his aircraft. If you have any ideas about Asia, speak to Junkers, he will be delighted" (1950, 2:395–96).

A few days later, on September 5, 1925, Hedin flew from south Sweden to Junkers's private airport in Germany. Junkers spent considerable time before the conference explaining to Hedin his plan to put in operation a regular air service from Germany to Peking, via the Soviet Union. His first move would be to fly three aircraft to China and exhibit them in major cities, to popularize the idea of air transport there. He added that if Hedin wanted to explore parts of Inner Asia, aircraft would be put at his disposal and Junkers would cover all his expenses. To Hedin, it was all unbelievable: "It was like a saga, an unlikely novel! I had to pinch myself to make certain I was awake, not dreaming" (1950, 2:396).

On his return to Stockholm, Hedin immediately set to work on a plan for this new expedition, designed mainly to lay the bases of an air connection between Germany and China. His long memorandum on the subject, dated October 1, 1925 (Manuscript in Riksarkiv, Stockholm), suggested that the air route surveyed by the expedition should lead from Berlin to Moscow, thence across the Ural Mountains, Siberia, and Mongolia to Peking. He reckoned the distance to be 7,825 kilometers. At an average airspeed of 150 kilometers per hour (100 miles per hour)—a respectable speed at that time—the flying time from Berlin to Peking would be fifty-two hours, he calculated. He described in detail every leg of the trip, including the eastbound as well as the westbound voyages, suggested locations for fuel depots and landing strips, and warned against severe climatic hazards, especially the wind and sandstorms of Chinese Central Asia.

Hedin pointed out that besides the then-unmapped areas that comprise the headwaters of the great rivers of East and Southeast Asia, a sizable part of northern Tibet remained unexplored. Overflights, he wrote, would provide information of exceptional importance on these areas, both for future air travel and for scientific work.

For the return journey of this expedition, Hedin suggested a route that would lead from Peking through the Chinese province of Sinkiang, Russian Central Asia, Iran, and Turkey, and back to Germany. In his calculations, he set the distance for the return journey at 10,450 kilometers, and the distance to be covered by flights for scientific purposes at 15,000 kilometers. He estimated that the time required for overflights for scientific work would be fifteen days. Such expeditions, Hedin wrote, would be of the greatest importance both for aviation and for scientific exploration, taking place at a watershed period between the age of caravans and the age of aircraft.

Three weeks after Hedin put down on paper his plan for the Central Asian expedition, he returned to Junkers's headquarters in Germany for further discussions. The plan appeared to be assured of success as long as Chinese and Russian permission for overflights could be secured.

During the winter of 1925–26, however, difficulties arose. The Junkers company's financial position was no longer secure, and in mid-1926 it was brought under the direct control of the German government. Hedin's dream of returning to Asia was threatened, but within a few months the project received support from a new sponsor, the German state airline, Deutsche Lufthansa. Hedin reopened negotiations with Lufthansa representatives, and in a very short time they reached agreement for an expedition to lay the groundwork for a Berlin-Peking air connection via Central Asia.

The most important task of the Lufthansa-sponsored expedition was to establish a small number of weather stations across western China. For that purpose, a German meteorologist, Waldemar Haude, was hired, and a group of German pilots, veterans of the First World War, were to join the expedition to help with ground surveys, pass judgment on potential landing sites, and direct the building of fuel and parts depots along the proposed air route. Haude, one of the first airline weather forecasters, was charged with the task of choosing five weather station sites between the Soviet-Chinese border in far western China and Peking and with training Chinese weather observers. Aircraft were to be brought to China, and flights were to begin within two years, by 1928 at the latest.

Haude, as meteorologist in charge, assembled the complex equipment for the weather stations, which filled forty large trunks. It was dispatched by train via Russia to Peking. In the meantime, Hedin assembled his staff, consisting of six Swedes, one Dane, eleven Germans, and ten Chinese (1937–, 23:xiii).

Hedin left Berlin in late October, 1926, traveling by the Trans-Siberian Railroad to Peking. But once there, his problems began. The Chinese at first objected even to the word expedition. In their view the term was used only to describe journeys to primitive

113

peoples. It took six months of negotiations with representatives of the Chinese government and Chinese scientific organizations to reach an agreement that was signed on April 26, 1927. Under its terms the undertaking was to be known as the Sino-Swedish Scientific Expedition, and officially it was to be led by a Chinese. The agreement imposed severe restrictions on Hedin: all archaeological finds were to be kept by China, only small-scale maps were to be made, and the scientific results were to be published in China.

Hedin, a veteran of negotiations with Chinese officials during his expeditions to Tibet, agreed to these restrictions, aware that the Chinese would be able to exercise little effective control. He was anxious to have his group get under way. It was a team of scientists and technicians; besides Hedin, Folke Bergman, archaeologist; Erik Norin, geologist; and David Hummel, physician and botanist, made up the scientific staff. All were Swedes. Two other Swedes, Frans Larson and Georg Söderbom, were engaged as field managers. Both had had long years of experience in China and Mongolia dealing with officials and local businesses.

Waldemar Haude, the meteorologist, came from Germany, and so did the nine pilots. Paul Lieberenz, the movie operator, was also from Germany. Hedin had insisted that a full pictorial record of the expedition be kept, both in stills and in moving pictures.

Writing the history of the expedition nearly fifteen years later, Hedin described his own role as

> connecting link and perambulating headquarters, as it were, watching over the interests of the expedition, and the many part-expeditions, with the Swedish and Chinese authorities. My headquarters were sometimes in Europe, sometimes in Asia or America. Stockholm, Urumchi, Peking, Nanking, and Chicago were during this period my most frequented resorts. (1937–, 23:xv)

For Hedin it was a completely new way of exploration. Having undertaken three major expeditions to Inner Asia earlier, in each case accompanied only by Asian servants and without any trained assistants, he now supervised the work of specialists in many fields, rather than making his own scientific observations. "During these years I learned . . . how much easier it is to cross the continent in different directions alone, with a few servants, than to lead a great expedition, a campaign of troops of five different nationalities," he wrote in his account of the expedition (1937–, 23:xix).

In May, 1927, having overcome Chinese resistance to his plans, Hedin and his group left Peking for Inner Mongolia to lay the groundwork for the proposed German-Chinese air connection. That aim, the basis of his support from Lufthansa, was never lost. Neither did Chinese opposition to the project let up, even for a short time. Six months after his departure from Peking, having reached Urumchi, the capital of Sinkiang, Hedin wrote to the Lufthansa executives in Berlin:

The educated Chinese here, and those in power, say to me: You pretend that the Germans provide 'planes for you only to give you a chance to carry out aerial surveys of unexplored desert. You want us to believe that? That poor Germany is spending these sums to allow you to look at the desert! No, the Germans have other aims, political ones. These cannot be achieved now. But in ten or twenty years, when Germany is a great power once again. . . . (April 4, 1928)

The Chinese authorities continued to refuse permission for overflights during the seven years the Sino-Swedish expedition operated in Chinese Central Asia. It was not until 1933 that the first German aircraft flew over the area and not until 1937 that the first flight between Berlin and the Chinese city of Sian took place.

During the remaining months of 1927, and in 1928, the expedition's work was carried on in many places. The main task, establishing the chain of weather stations and surveying the terrain for possible landing sites, went on, but at the same time archaeological, botanical, geological, geodetic, and ethnographic studies were also undertaken. Hedin acted as overseer, diplomat, expediter, and fund-raiser while his staff collected a considerable body of valuable scientific information.

In May, 1928, Lufthansa showed signs of impatience, since the Chinese were still not permitting overflights. It became apparent to Hedin that in order to continue the valuable scientific investigations that were going on in Chinese territory he had to look for funds elsewhere. In May, 1928, he returned to Sweden and lobbied for government support for his expedition. Confident that he could count on Swedish government funds, he returned to China, only to find that during his absence the governor of the province of Sinkiang, main base of the expedition, had been assassinated; the new governor was strongly opposed to continuing the expedition's work.

The 1920s and 1930s, when the Sino-Swedish expedition was working in western and southwestern China, were times of trouble in China. Civil war raged intermittently in most of the provinces. Peking, the traditional capital, was supplanted by Nanking as the official capital of the country, but scientific institutions continued to function in the old capital as before. And the long shadow of Japan, intent on taking advantage of China's unsettled condition and bent on extending its control over parts of the country, hovered over the horizon. Hedin had no choice, however; for the expedition to continue its work, it needed the support of the central government, and he journeyed in late spring of 1929 to Nanking. Chiang Kai-shek, the de facto head of China's central government, promised his cooperation, and Hedin went on to Peking confident that he could return to Central Asia with the government's blessing.

As it turned out, his plans had to be completely changed. While in Peking, in June, 1929, he became very ill, and physicians diagnosed his illness as a tumor in his spinal cord. He was advised to seek the views of Harvey Cushing, one of the world's outstanding neurosurgeons, and Hedin traveled to Cushing's office in Boston. To his immense relief, Cushing's diagnosis was totally different from that of the physicians in Peking; he sent a telegram to Peking saying that "practical absence of physical symptoms makes me hesitate to accept diagnosis" (1950, 2:425).

Hedin's 1929 journey to America had another, equally important, result. While in the United States, he met Vincent Bendix, a wealthy Chicago industrialist of Swedish origin, and succeeded in getting him interested in his expedition. Hedin had hoped to acquire a Chinese lama temple for the Stockholm Museum of Ethnography, and the project appealed to Bendix. "I guess I can contribute to your plans for the acquisition of a lama temple and ethnographic collections with as big a sum as you had from the Swedish government. Not much difficulty in that" (1937–, 24:62–63). Bendix's contribution actually amounted to twice the sum Hedin had received from the Swedish government.

Two lama temples were to be acquired or copied, under the agreement with Mr. Bendix, one for Chicago and one for Stockholm, and both were to be completely equipped, with everything in the way of images, cult-objects, textiles, robes, musical instruments, etc., that belonged to the interior and exterior decoration. If anything were left over from the sum donated, it was to be used to purchase ethnographical objects, that should be equally divided between the museums of both cities. (1937–, 24:62–63)

Once more Hedin returned to Peking. He remained there for over a year, from October, 1929, to January, 1931. He was a public relations manager, a diplomat negotiating with the Chinese authorities, and the overall director for the expedition. In this, the expedition's second phase, which lasted from late 1928 to 1933, the number of participants increased. Eight more Swedes joined the staff, in addition to two Danes, an Estonian, and several Germans and Chinese (1937–, 24:xi). Expenses were shared by the Swedish government, Lufthansa, Vincent Bendix, and Hedin himself (1937–, 23:xiv–xv).

It was during this second phase, in June, 1930, that Hedin, accompanied by several members of the expedition staff, traveled to the old imperial city of Jehol, north of Peking, in his search for a temple to be copied and shipped to America. Jehol had been the favorite summer resdience of the two greatest rulers of the Manchu Dynasty, the emperors K'ang-hsi (1654–1722) and Ch'ien-lung (1736–96). Visitors who had seen Jehol in its age of splendor, in the eighteenth and nineteenth centuries, had described it as a Chinese Versailles, a great complex of palaces, temples, and gardens where emperors spent part of the year and received visiting rulers and ambassadors, among them King George III of England's ambassador, Lord Macartney, in 1793.

Hedin's choice was the so-called Golden Pavilion, built in the 1760s. It was part of the complex that was known as Potala because of its resemblance to the residence of the Dalai Lama in Lhasa. In a beautifully illustrated book, *Jehol, Imperial City*, Hedin described the Golden Pavilion as

> a pearl of Chinese architecture, once the most beautiful lama temple in China. The double roofs were covered with sheet copper, gilded with dull gold. Their corners curved upwards, a characteristic of Chinese roof-architecture which gave the building a rhythmic, billowing charm. (1937–, 24:128ff)

He commissioned a Chinese architect to build an exact replica of the Golden Pavilion; it was completely furnished with hangings, altars, statues, all of the necessary furnishings of a lama temple in use. It was shipped in crates to Chicago and exhibited at the 1933 World's Fair; it was dismantled and then rebuilt for the New York World's Fair of 1939. It was dismantled again in 1940 and is still in storage, but it is to be reconstructed as part of the Museum of Oriental Art at Indiana University in Bloomington.

In February, 1932, Hedin traveled to Chicago to oversee the construction of the Golden Pavilion and stayed in America until December of that year. He then returned to Peking, where the Sino-Swedish expedition was about to complete its work. The expedition, whose original purpose had been to survey the Chinese segment of the proposed Berlin-Peking air route across northwestern and western China, had taken a different tack because of the Chinese government's reluctance to grant permission for actual flights. Both the purpose of the expedition and the area in which it operated were fundamentally changed. The project became a many-sided scientific undertaking, and the area of its work included the whole of innermost Asia, from the Chinese-Soviet frontier in the north to western Tibet in the south, from the high mountains of Karakoram in westernmost China to the borders of what was then called China proper (1937–, 23:56).

By early summer, 1933, Hedin was ready to wind up operations in China, but a new project began to take shape. In June, 1933, he was a guest at a dinner given by the German minister to China, and there met the deputy foreign minister of the Chinese government. Western China was in a state of civil war, and the central government was eager to regain control of that distant area. Hedin suggested that motor roads should be built to Sinkiang province, the area of greatest concern. The minister found the idea eminently practical and suggested that Hedin accept leadership of a small, motorized expedition to survey such a road.

Plans for this survey were completed by late summer. The expedition was to be undertaken on behalf of the Chinese government and at its expense. Hedin was in charge, with the title of Adviser to the Ministry of Railways; his task was "to investigate, and to submit to the Government [of China] proposals concerning the laying of two motor-car roads, between China Proper and the province of Sinkiang" (1937–, 23:xv). He was authorized to take with him a staff consisting of Chinese and Swedish specialists.

Hedin enlisted Dr. David Hummel, physician and botanist, who had participated in the earlier phases of the Sino-Swedish Expedition; Folke Bergman, an archaeologist and also a veteran of the expedition; Georg Söderbom, who had been field manager of the expedition; and a young Swede then living in Peking, Efraim Hill, as driver. Parker Chen, a Chinese geodesist, and two Chinese engineers completed Hedin's small staff.

In the discussions Hedin held with Chinese government officials, it was agreed that the survey would include a traverse from the westernmost Chinese railhead then in existence to the capital of Sinkiang province, Urumchi. Beyond that point, three alternate roads were to be reconnoitered, leading from Urumchi to the Sino-Soviet border, to the Tarim Basin, and to the furthest Chinese town of importance in that basin, Kashgar. Much of this territory had been well known to Hedin since he entered China more than forty years earlier. His view of the problems of transportation in westernmost China was clear-cut: he advocated building roads first and railroads later. In the years since 1933, his suggestions have been closely followed: today Sinkiang is linked to the main part of China both by roads and by a railroad.

On October 21, 1933, Hedin and his staff left Peking for the northwest. By February, 1934, their convoy of two cars and three trucks, traveling over bad roads that were often only caravan trails, reached the eastern part of Sinkiang province. The local warlord who had controlled Sinkiang for several years, General Ma, nicknamed Big Horse, was then under attack, and his forces were retreating toward the Tarim Basin to the southwest. Hedin and his staff had the misfortune of finding themselves in the path of General Ma's retreat. At one time they were put under arrest and threatened with execution unless they placed the vehicles of the expedition at the general's disposal. Hedin, then in his late sixties, was treated as roughly as his staff, but showed extraordinary courage in standing up to his captors, making only minimal concessions even when he believed he and his companions were to be shot.

That adventure, which took place in the town of Korla, was but one of a string of mishaps that befell Hedin and his small group, mishaps that included house arrest, temporary confiscation of their cars and trucks, shortfalls of food and automotive fuel, and illness. Nevertheless, the group managed to travel far and wide across Sinkiang, even visiting the Wandering Lake, Lop Nor, which Hedin had first observed on his journey to this part of western China in 1890.

On February 7, 1935, after being gone for sixteen months, Hedin and his companions reached the railhead in Sian. Later that month he made his report to the Railway Ministry in Nanking and was decorated by the Chinese government for his labors.

A few weeks later, on April 15, 1935, Hedin returned to Stockholm. It was, he wrote in his history of the expedition, nearly nine years from the time he first had left his native city for Peking. For

Hedin it was the crowning event of his fifty years of exploration; for the scientific staff of the great expedition it had meant many years of fruitful work published in an extraordinary series of monographs, *Reports from the Scientific Expedition to the Northwestern Provinces of China, under the Leadership of Dr. Sven Hedin—The Sino-Swedish Expedition.* It comprises fifty-four volumes so far, the first published in 1937 and the most recent in 1982. These publications fall into nine categories: geography, geology, paleobotany, invertebrate paleontology, archaeology, ethnography, meteorology, zoology, and botany. Besides writing introductions and prefaces, Hedin contributed three volumes totaling 877 pages on the history of the expedition from 1927 to 1935.

Between 1931 and 1940, Hedin also wrote four books for the general reader, describing his own and his staff's adventures in China: *Across the Gobi Desert, Riddles of the Gobi Desert, Big Horse's Flight* (dealing with General Ma, the warlord of Sinkiang), and *The Silk Road.* In their English versions, these books total over 1,300 pages. Originally published in Swedish, they also appeared in German, Dutch, Czech, Latvian, Danish, Italian, Hungarian, Japanese, Turkish, and in one instance in Chinese. Much of Hedin's income from these books went to cover part of the expenses of the expedition.

The *Reports from the Scientific Expedition* were written by members of the expedition, but other scholars, both Swedish and German, contributed to a number of the volumes. Together, the volumes represent a unique and monumental contribution to our knowledge of western China, Mongolia, and Tibet. Their value does not lie only in the fact that Hedin's 1926–35 venture was the last to be led by a European and staffed almost entirely by Europeans. The uniformly high scholarship of the authors, the wealth of illustrations, and the scientific detachment from any political or racial prejudice makes the *Reports* among the most important European contributions to our knowledge of the geology, paleontology, zoology, botany, and ethnology of Inner Asia.

Hedin had been enthusiastic about the possibility offered by Hugo Junkers's project, a survey of an air route across Asia. But his dream of exploring from the air the little-known mountain and river systems of southwesternmost China could not be translated into reality. During most of the years the expedition was in the field, Chinese opposition to any overflight made it impossible. Instead, the scientists Hedin engaged as participants returned with an extraordinary harvest of observations that has taken over forty years to be presented to the world of scholars and whose publication is not yet complete. Together with *Southern Tibet,* the *Reports from the Scientific Expedition* are Sven Hedin's true monument.

Writing in the Swedish geographical journal *Geografiska Annaler* in 1954, two years after Hedin's death, Erik Norin, senior geologist of the expedition, tried to explain why Hedin, a man who undertook three great expeditions to the wilderness of Inner Asia without any European companions, decided to make this, his last, a group venture. Norin was of the opinion that Hedin had long preferred to go it alone because he wanted to set his own pace, decide the route he wanted to follow, and above all not risk any other man's life, only his own. Having contributed so much to the knowledge of Inner Asia in his earlier travels, he was convinced that further work needed experts in several specialized fields to carry out scientific investigations in depth.

> Although the individual scientists enjoyed a great deal of freedom in the choice of their field of investigation, and each managed to work independently of the others, the expedition was a single organic, effective unit, where every group followed the research task set by the Chief. . . . He allowed us fruitful and fascinating research in what was often untouched terrain, while he undertook the often hopeless-seeming task of smoothing the way for us through all the political and economic difficulties the expedition had to contend with. (Norin 1954, 39)

Hedin's skill in negotiating with Chinese officials impressed his staff deeply. Gösta Montell, ethnographer and anthropologist, who was Hedin's closest collaborator during the last years of his life, wrote:

He had unfailing tact in the company of all sorts of people. His personal charm was a great advantage in all his transactions with stubborn mandarins and ill-disposed lamas. Indeed, I cannot imagine anything that could have seriously put him off his balance and I cannot remember a single occasion when he lost his self control, however trying the situation. (Montell 1954, 8)

XIII

Diplomat behind the Scenes, 1935–44

The years Hedin spent in Inner Asia, between 1926 and 1935, brought major changes in the world. He was aware of the Great Depression of the 1930s, since it had a direct impact on the finances of his China expedition, and he knew that fascism, already firmly installed in Italy, triumphed in Germany in 1933. The decade between his return from China in 1935 and the end of the Second World War saw Hedin once more active in the political arena—this time, however, he participated not just in Swedish internal politics but in world affairs as well.

In one of his last books, published in Sweden in 1949 with the title *On Unofficial Mission in Berlin,* and published two years later in Dublin in English translation with the title *Sven Hedin's German Diary, 1935–1942,* Hedin wrote a detailed account of his contacts with the leaders of the "new Germany," the "Thousand-Year Reich" that was created on January 30, 1933, when the president of the German Republic, Hindenburg, appointed as chancellor the leader of the National Socialist Workers' Party, Adolf Hitler. In August, 1934, after Hindenburg's death, Hitler become both president and chancellor of Germany, and the Nazi party proceeded to remake Germany in its own image.

Hedin had several indirect contacts with Hitler. In October, 1933, Hitler sent a telegram congratulating him on the fortieth anniversary of his first expedition to Inner Asia; in 1935, Hedin received a congratulatory telegram from Hitler on his seventieth birthday; and on his return journey from China that same year via Russia and Germany, Hitler sent several officials of the Chancellery to greet him at the railroad station in Berlin. But he met Hitler in person for the first time in October, 1935.

The occasion of that meeting was Hedin's journey to Germany to give a lecture tour. On his return from China, Hedin was in need of a considerable sum . . . to set in hand at once the working up of the vast material, in the form of collections and notes accumulated during our eight years in Asia by every member of my staff of scholars. (1949, 7)

He had made lecture tours of Germany several times before, and he had always been extraordinarily popular as a public speaker. His talks, given in concert halls and large auditoriums, attracted thousands of listeners, and his fees were usually very high. He noted in his diary that on this tour he gave 130 public lectures during his travels, in ninety-one cities in Germany, Austria, Hungary, Czechoslovakia, Switzerland, the Netherlands, and Denmark. The tour was impressive by any standards, even more so when it is remembered that Sven Hedin was seventy years old at the time.

Eric Wennerholm, Hedin's attorney and close friend, recalls Hedin's description of the tour:

I felt like a circus horse. . . . Seldom were my marches in the desert as demanding as this tour. . . . But those marches cost money, and the lectures provided big money, indispensable funds. (Wennerholm 1978, 244–45)

It was at the beginning of the lecture tour, in Berlin, on October 9, 1935, that Hedin met Hitler. He was visiting Hermann Göring, chief of the German Air Force, and Göring took him to Hitler's office. Hitler met Hedin with open arms, saying, "At last we meet, Herr Doktor!" Hedin's description of the conversation reveals his feelings about the Führer.

He did all the talking himself almost the whole time, describing in clear and strong words the goals of National Socialism, and his efforts to raise up Germany and her people from the humiliation that was done in Versailles, and from the morass in which the Germans had been struggling under the dull and weak government of the Weimar Republic. In strong words, he set forth the principles of the new organization and spoke with evident satisfaction of the determination and enthusiasm with which youth were being brought up to be new, hard-working and useful people. The German people were with him in the principle: one people, one country, one leader, and no one doubted a bright future. "There is feverish activity everywhere, unemployment is being wiped out, I would like to show you everything myself, but I must stay at my post, and time is short!" (1949, 8–9)

Writing about Germany a short time later, Hedin described the reasons for his great interest in the new German regime.

When I came home in mid-April, 1935, something was happening in Germany. Only confused news reached Inner Asia. Everything was new to me. All my experience, all my memories were from the days of the Weimar Republic. I looked upon the new world view and the reorganization, characteristic of the National Socialists and their victorious leader, with scepticism. I found it hard to believe in the possibility of so radically changing a people that had traditions two thousand years old. I undertook my study of the men of this new era with the same curiosity and excitement that I had known when I visited the lands of the Kirghiz, the Mongols, the Tibetans. I returned home with the idea of a rest, intending to work on scientific materials. Instead I embarked on a voyage of discovery in terra incognita, located south of our own country. One thing was certain: there was going to be a book describing this voyage. (1937, 9–10)

Toward the end of his 1935–36 lecture tour, Hedin called on Walter Funk, secretary of state in the Nazi Ministry for Propaganda, and announced that he wanted to write a book on the new Germany (1949, 8–9). Funk was enchanted by the possible major propaganda coup: a world-famous explorer, lifelong supporter of all things German, was ready to describe the Third Reich. Funk and his chief, Nazi Propaganda Minister Joseph Goebbels, welcomed the opportunity.

Their first move was to invite Hedin to be one of the four speakers at the opening of the 1936 Olympic Games in Berlin. There were to have been four speakers, one each from Europe, North America, Africa, and Asia, but Hedin was the only one to accept the invitation. He delivered his formal address in the Berlin Olympic Stadium, beginning with the words "I call on the youth of the world!" The speech was a great success, and Hedin was asked to Hitler's box to accept the führer's personal congratulations (Diary, August 4, 1936).

By the fall of 1936, arrangements in Germany were completed. Hedin was to come to Germany as a guest of the government to find out first hand about the Third Reich. He was installed in the private residence of a German industrialist, who placed his house at Hedin's disposal, complete with domestic servants and automobile. For the next several weeks, Hedin was visited daily by an official of the Propaganda Ministry, Wilhelm Ziegler. Hedin refers to him as his

> teacher, who was to direct my studies in the doctrines and views of National Socialism. He piled the table with stacks of books and brochures, marked all the passages I ought to read, and delivered lectures on which I made notes. (1949, 13)

Later, Hedin traveled, always accompanied by someone from the Propaganda Ministry, to a number of places in Germany, "to centers of industry and labor, where we were always shown round by local experts" (1949, 13). After such a heavy dose of indoctrination, Goebbels and the other members of the Nazi hierarchy expected a book full of praise. But on receiving Hedin's manuscript in April, 1937, Secretary of State Funk informed him that unless changes were made, the book could not be published in Germany (1949, 17).

The Nazis objected to the contents and tone of two chapters dealing with the Nazi attitude toward science and toward Jews in Germany. In Hedin's view, science is international, regardless of political boundaries and world views. One cannot say that the Third Reich has one kind of science and Soviet Russia another, and that both are different from what the rest of the world calls science. Science is and must be fully free, a search after eternal truth, regardless of the constantly changing political winds. Research that is not free . . . is not what scholars call science. (1937, 245)

In his chapter on Jews, Hedin agreed with the Nazi contention that Jews occupied a place out of proportion to their numbers in Germany in the theater, the press, law, and medicine.

But one must ask, could a less radical solution of this seemingly insoluble problem be found? Would it not have been wiser and more just to limit cleansing to that element which in fact damaged Germany, through its destructive role in politics and literature, that forced itself to posts that by right belonged to Germans? (1937, 272)

After a lengthy correspondence with the Nazi Propaganda Ministry, in which Hedin made it clear that he would not delete any part of his manuscript, the book did appear in Sweden, entitled *Germany and World Peace,* in May, 1937, but not in Germany. A few days later Hedin received a letter from Hitler complimenting him on his book. But there was no mention of its publication in Germany, and that was the end of that story.

In 1937, 1938, and 1939 Hedin worked in Stockholm directing the publication of the scientific results of the China expedition. His diary records his awareness of world affairs and his fear of the constant drift toward yet another major war. A few days after the Munich conference that decided the dismemberment of Czechoslovakia, he listened to a speech Hitler made in the city of Saarbrücken near the French frontier. Hedin felt that the speech was harmful to Germany, that Hitler was driving the Western powers and the Soviets towards rearmament. "If he would only ask my views as a friend of Germany," he wrote in his diary, "I would tell him what I think and show him the way to greatness" (October 10, 1938).

On August 23, 1939, Germany and the Soviet Union signed a nonaggression pact. Ten days later, after the German invasion of Poland, the Second World War began. Sweden remained neutral, and Hedin followed closely the course of the war and its possible extension into Scandinavia. Under the terms of the German-Russian pact, the Soviets were given free hand in the three Baltic republics, Estonia, Latvia, and Lithuania, and in late September and early October, the Soviet Union established military bases on their territory. It was only a question of time before similar Soviet demands were made on Finland. Hedin, always aware of the Russian danger to Sweden were Finland to be under Russian rule or even influence, became convinced that he might obtain German support for Finland.

An entry in Hedin's diary recorded his idea.

I suddenly had the notion to go to Berlin, to talk with Hitler about Sweden's and Finland's position. I suppose you could look on this as self-inspired and self-righteous, that a man, singled out in Sweden as a Nazi sympathizer, who furthermore is almost blind, without official mission and during a violent war, should negotiate with a belligerent power. (October 13, 1939)

On October 14, 1939, Sven Hedin arrived in Berlin accompanied by his sister Alma, who acted as his secretary.

The next day, Hedin was received by Göring, chief of the German Air Force. In the course of a discussion on world affairs, he assured Hedin of German victory in the end. On October 16, Hedin was received by Hitler at his office. The conversation was about Finland. Hitler assured his visitor of German neutrality if there were a Soviet attack on Finland, even if Sweden chose to intervene in that conflict. Hedin asked the führer:

Without any authority and entirely on my own initiative, I take the liberty of asking you, Herr Reichskanzler, whether you would agree to a peace conference negotiated by the King of Sweden?

Hitler replied:

Yes, provided that England abandon her mad notion of the restoration of Czechoslovakia, and, second, that England recognize that the solution of the Polish question is a matter concerning solely Germany and Russia. (1949, 56)

After his conversation with Hitler, Hedin sat down with the secretary of state for the Chancellor's Office, Meissner, who dictated a memorandum regarding Hitler's views. Hedin always insisted that he had no official standing, but the official history of Swedish foreign policy during the Second World War presents a different view. According to that source,

It appears that the King [Gustav V of Sweden] asked Hedin to explore with Hitler prospects for the King acting as a convener of a peace conference which, if all went well, would be held in Stockholm. (Carlgren 1973, 48n.48).

The German authorities insisted that the conversation with Hitler should be reported only to King Gustav V. On his return from Berlin on October 18, Hedin got off the train in a suburb of Stockholm to evade reporters, drove directly to the royal palace, and gave a full report to the King and to Crown Prince Gustav Adolf. Later he informed the German legation in Stockholm that he followed his instructions and that only King Gustav V had read the memorandum dictated to Hedin in Berlin (Diary, October 29, 1939).

Six weeks after Hedin's visit to Berlin, on November 30, 1939, the Soviet Union attacked Finland after the Finnish government rejected Soviet demands for military bases on Finnish territory. The Finns fought valiantly, and public opinion in Sweden and throughout the world was in their favor, but there was little doubt about the outcome of the war.

Once more Hedin traveled to Berlin, and on March 4, 1940, was received by Hitler. The Finnish war was in its final phase, yet Hitler refused to discuss German intervention on Finland's behalf, not wishing to jeopardize German-Soviet relations (1949, 56). Hitler's views were restated in even stronger terms by his propaganda chief, Goebbels. When Hedin saw him on March 11, 1940, Goebbels said that "there is at present no likelihood that Germany would undertake such an intervention [on Finland's behalf], in a matter of no concern to us, that could endanger our friendship with Russia" (1949, 112). The next day, while Hedin was still in Berlin, word was received that Finland and the Soviet Union had signed an armistice.

During his stay in Berlin in March, 1940, Hedin met a number of Nazi leaders, among them the chiefs of the German Army and Navy. He also made the acquaintance of a German anthropologist, Ernst Schaefer, who had worked in Central Asia and actually visited Lhasa. Schaefer was a protégé of the head of the German SS organization, Heinrich Himmler, and was destined to cross Hedin's path again somewhat later, when he was director of his own institute for research in Central Asia.

In November and December of 1940, Hedin made one more trip to Berlin and was again received by Hitler. Vyacheslav Molotov, Soviet foreign minister, had just left Berlin after a visit during which he had informed the German leaders of Stalin's plans for Soviet expansion. According to Hedin, Hitler gave him assurances that although Molotov had made far-reaching demands on Finnish territory,

> I gave him to understand very clearly that further Russian occupation of Finnish territory was not in accordance with Germany's wishes. In the present situation, Finland has nothing to fear from the East and Sweden can be at rest. (1949, 199–209)

Hitler's statement that Sweden "can be at rest" would have struck someone less sympathetic to Germany than Hedin as not very reassuring. Nine months earlier, in April, 1940, German forces had invaded Denmark and Norway and within a few weeks both were under German military occupation. The reaction in those countries to a foreign occupier was almost immediate, and anti-German resistance forces were quickly organized. During the summer and fall of 1940, Germany, not content with full military occupation of Norway and Denmark, kept insisting that the Swedish government withdraw its recognition of the Norwegian legation in Stockholm.

Sweden had already accepted significant German demands, such as the transit of German troops across Sweden en route to Norway. But there was strong sympathy for Norway in Sweden, and a gesture denying it the privileges of diplomatic status was likely to result in a public outcry. Accordingly, one may assume, Hedin was asked to take up the matter of the status of Norwegian diplomats with the German leaders when he traveled to Berlin in November, 1940.

It was during his meeting with the German foreign minister, von Ribbentrop, that Hedin brought up the subject. Ribbentrop turned out to be in a talkative mood that day, and he outlined German war plans against England in considerable detail, possibly to convince Hedin, and through him Sweden's government, that German victory was inevitable. Ribbentrop insisted that the conversation remain secret, but assured Hedin that Germany would not insist any further on the matter of Norwegian diplomats in Sweden (1949, 215–29).

After his several visits to Berlin, Hedin became convinced that he was an important diplomatic personage. In April, 1941, reflecting in his diary on the events that had taken place since his return from China six years earlier, he took satisfaction from the fact that during those years he had published six books and given many lectures, but "the most important thing I had accomplished were my negotiations with Hitler" (April 15, 1941).

Hedin's view of his own role was only strengthened by the opinions of his friends. Thus, when he was entertained in the home of the Finnish minister to Sweden in January, 1941, he was informed that the Finnish government had awarded him the Order of the White Rose, the highest decoration Finland could offer a foreigner. His host added, "We want Russia to know that you are our friend, who speaks for Finland with Hitler!" (Diary, January 31, 1941).

During the spring of 1941, the war continued to spread across Europe, engulfing Yugoslavia and Greece. Sweden was a neutral island in the Nazi-dominated continent. It continued to follow the course of the war very closely and to express sympathy for its Scandinavian neighbors under foreign military occupation. When a German military court condemned thirteen Norwegian members of the Resistance to death in March, 1941, Swedish public opinion ran strongly in their favor. Hedin was approached from Norway and asked to intervene directly with the German authorities to obtain a commutation of the death sentences.

On April 4, 1941, Hedin wrote General Falkenhorst, commander-in-chief of German forces in Norway. The condemned Norwegians were considered true patriots, not only in Norway but throughout Scandinavia, wrote Hedin, and their execution would only hurt German prestige. Falkenhorst replied that only Hitler could change the death sentences to imprisonment and at the same time forwarded Hedin's letter to Berlin. Hitler did commute the death sentences to prison terms. In a letter written in 1946, the Norwegian lawyer who had defended several of the men accused before the German military court stated unequivocally that it was Hedin's request for clemency, coming from "a man who had a very good reputation with Hitler," that saved the lives of the thirteen Norwegians (1949, 232–46).

A short time after the issue of the Norwegian resistance fighters arose, Hedin was visited in Stockholm by an official of the German Foreign Office, Grassmann, a man with strong family ties in Sweden. He brought to Hedin suggestions coming, Hedin supposed, from the highest levels of the German government. It was suggested that Hedin should make a trip to the United States, at that time still a nonbelligerent nation. As a citizen of a neutral country, Hedin could make the journey via Lisbon, flying on an American airline. He should give lectures at American universities as the ostensible purpose of his trip. What Germany was really hoping for was that Hedin, a prestigious figure in world affairs as

134

far as it was concerned, should, during his stay in the United States, contact American leaders, those of the "America First" movement in particular, give press interviews, and stress the importance of a continuing nonbelligerent policy for America. It was hoped that he would also speak on American radio on the same theme (Diary, April 22, 1941).

Hedin declined, citing his age, his status as a citizen of a neutral country, his conviction that the United States was going to enter the war sooner or later, and his view that the United States was a de facto participant in the war already, since it was sending aid to Germany's enemies (1949, 249–50).

Germany was determined to take advantage of Hedin's support of its war aims, however, and a month later, on May 22, 1941, the same Foreign Office representative returned to Stockholm with another idea. This time, it was the notion that a book stating Hedin's views on the United States and American neutrality was likely to have considerable influence in America. The book was to contain Hedin's own reminiscences on his visits to the United States on earlier occasions, in 1923, 1929, and 1932. It was to include excerpts from speeches by prominent Americans who opposed American entry in the war, men of the caliber of former President Hoover, Colonel Charles Lindbergh, and Senators Borah and Wheeler. The book would also discuss results of public opinion polls taken since the beginning of the war in the United States; information on problems of the American economy and the effect of the war on it; views on what the world would be like after the war, especially emphasizing the worldwide misery that would result from a German defeat and would push Europe back to the darkest of the Middle Ages. The final thrust of the book, the German authorities believed, should be that if the United States remained neutral, at least one continent would be spared the ravages of war and would remain a haven of peace, and the place where reconstruction of the postwar world could begin (Diary, May 22, 1941).

The idea of such a book appealed to Hedin. Within a few weeks Grassmann returned, this time accompanied by a Foreign Office specialist in American affairs, Gärtner. Grassmann and

Gärtner acted as Hedin's secretary and research assistant in the preparation of the book. The manuscript was finished in less than a month; the two Germans spent long hours in Hedin's apartment helping to compile the material (Diary, July 14, 1941). The next problem was to get the manuscript to an American publisher. Pan American Airways maintained regular flights between Portugal and the United States, and it would have been easy to get the manuscript to Portugal across German-occupied Europe. But the Lisbon–to–New York flights touched down at Bermuda, where British censorship of transatlantic mail was known to be strict and efficient.

At this time, the Hearst newspaper group's Stockholm-based Scandinavian correspondent got wind of the existence of a book strongly advocating American neutrality, a view then supported by the Hearst papers. King Features Syndicate, a part of the Hearst group, informed Hedin that they were interested in the book but could not make a decision without seeing the manuscript (Diary, August 23, 1941). On receiving that information Dr. A. Draeger, an official of the German Propaganda Ministry, informed Hedin that "it would be very nice if Hearst agreed and you would cable the entire manuscript. As you already know, we will look after expenses at this end (Letter from A. Draeger, August 22, 1941).

Negotiations continued without the manuscript being sent to America until, in December, 1941, the United States entered the war and its publication there became impossible. Instead, it was first published in Germany in 1942, with the title *America in the Struggle between Continents*. French, Dutch, Serbian, Czech, and Spanish versions appeared in 1943, and the original Swedish text was published in 1944.

Hedin sent a copy of the book to Adolf Hitler with a personal inscription. In return he received a long letter praising the book and agreeing with the author that "the man personally responsible for this war, as you so correctly state at the end of the book, is the American president, Roosevelt" (Hitler, October 30, 1942).

In 1942 the war was still going in Germany's favor, or so it seemed in the eyes of Germany's supporters. In mid-May of 1942,

Hedin traveled once more to Berlin, ostensibly to give a formal lecture but secretly hoping that he could meet with Hitler and plead for more lenient treatment of Norway. But he could not obtain an audience and returned, discouraged, to Sweden. Yet this trip was truly signficiant in another respect: Hedin, using his influence with top Nazi officials, was able to save the life of one of Germany's distinguished scholars, Alfred Philippson.

Philippson was a contemporary of Hedin's, and the two had been friends and fellow students of Richthofen in Berlin half a century earlier. Philippson, who was Jewish, had had a brilliant university career, had held one of the most prestigious posts in German geography, at the University of Bonn, and had been recognized by the government of Prussia with the title of Privy Councillor in 1915. He had retired in 1929 but continued to travel and write, especially about the lands of the Mediterranean. As a man with worldwide reputation, he was able to continue to publish his studies in German professional journals even after the Nazi takeover, and in 1933 he was honored by the Berlin Geographical Society with its Richthofen gold medal. Soon after that, however, the Nazi laws against Jews were applied to him: he could no longer publish his work in Germany, and after 1938, his passport was withdrawn and he could no longer travel. After the outbreak of war in 1939, Philippson, his wife, and his daughter were forced to leave their home. Together with two other prominent Jewish citizens of Bonn, they were interned in a closely watched building in the city. In mid-June, 1942, the two leading geography professors at the University of Bonn, Troll and Meinardus, found out that Philippson and his family were about to be "transported to the East," the euphemism for deportation to the death camps in Poland.

Professor Troll knew that Hedin was in Germany at the time and after considerable difficulty reached him in his hotel in Berlin to inform him that his old school friend was about to leave Bonn the next morning. "This is your last chance," Troll said to Hedin, "you must speak to Frick, Minister of the Interior, tomorrow morning."

Hedin did speak to the Minister of the Interior, and Philippson and his family were given a reprieve. Instead of being deported to the death camps they spent the remaining years of the war in a Nazi concentration camp for special prisoners, in Theresienstadt-Terezin in Czechoslovakia. Philippson returned to Bonn in 1945 and spent the last eight years of his life in his home, continuing to work until the end of his long and illustrious career. Hedin thus knew that his close relationship with the leaders of Nazi Germany had enabled him to save the life of his old friend and fellow geographer (Carl Troll, personal communication with author, 1967).

On January 8, 1943, Hedin left Stockholm on his last trip to Germany. He had been informed some months earlier that Himmler, the SS chief, had decided to create an Institute of Central Asian Studies at the University of Munich and name it after Hedin. As the rector of the university put it, the new Sven Hedin Institute of Central Asian Studies was to preserve forever Hedin's name as an explorer of Inner Asia, the man who filled in the last unknown spots on the map of Asia (Diary, June 10, 1942).

Arriving in Berlin, Hedin was a guest at a dinner honoring German Air Force chief Göring on his fiftieth birthday. He then traveled on to Munich and was present at the official opening of the Hedin Institute. His prestige in Germany had never been greater. His books continued to be best-sellers and brought in such sums that, as he wrote in his diary, his royalties from Germany were the highest ever in his fifty years of working with the Brockhaus publishing firm (Diary, July 9, 1943).

Back in Sweden, Hedin returned to his desk to continue his work. Besides supervising publication of the results of his last expedition, he also managed to write an elegant book on Swedish landscapes, based on his travels. On October 5, 1944, he was received by King Gustav V, to whom he presented a copy of his new book. The outcome of the war was no longer in doubt. Allied landings in Normandy in June, 1944, led to the liberation of France, and in the east, Russian forces were approaching German territory. But Hedin refused even to consider German defeat and said so in his conversation with the king.

King Gustav V, who had always supported the German point of

view, told Hedin that he found Germany's actions "truly barbarian" and that he could not understand how Hedin still believed in the final victory of Germany. "For the longest time I did believe in Germany," said King Gustav, "but I cannot do so any longer" (Diary, October 5, 1944). A few days later, Hedin met Crown Prince Gustav Adolf, to whom he spoke of Hitler's promise, made in 1939, that "Sweden had nothing to fear." The crown prince reminded him of earlier promises that Hitler had not kept and expressed his belief that while there had been danger for Sweden in 1940, when Germany had just completed the conquest of Norway and Denmark, he saw no danger for Sweden were Germany to lose the war (Diary, October 10, 1944).

On February 19, 1945, Sven Hedin turned eighty. Congratulatory telegrams came from hundreds of people; even the leaders of Nazi Germany, then in its final days, remembered the occasion. A few weeks later, the war in Europe ended with the surrender of German forces. When the staff of the German legation left Stockholm to return home, only two people watched their departure on the waterfront in Stockholm harbor, Hedin and a young newspaper reporter. Later he wrote in his diary, "Two world wars in one lifetime are too many" (Wennerholm 1978, 268).

XIV

Reaping the Harvest of Years, 1945–52

The collapse of Germany in 1945 meant the collapse of an important part of Hedin's world. This time, the defeat was complete: the terms were those of unconditional surrender. For Hedin, the loss was not only that of a country he loved, where some of his greatest triumphs had taken place, but a financial loss, too. For more than fifty years, his private finances had depended largely on royalties from his books published in Germany (1949, 26).

Yet Hedin did not simply pull back into the comfort of his apartment overlooking Stockholm's Lake Mälar, to brood over the past. He had turned eighty in February, 1945; shortly afterward he called his lawyer and financial adviser, Eric Wennerholm, to his home. His question was blunt and to the point. "Tell me," he said to Wennerholm, "just how much do we have, how much can I expect in royalties from my books, how much would that amount to for a year? What I want to know is this: how long would that last me?"

The two men looked at the figures and came up with five years. "Five years, but that is ridiculous! Papa lived to be 91, Mama, 87. Looks as if I must start to work again, not just scientific stuff but popular books as well, that bring in money. I have lots of ideas" (Wennerholm 1978, 273–74).

Hedin did have a lot of ideas, and writing was never a hardship for him. In the last full year of the war, 1944, he published three books of his own and also wrote the third and last volume of the history of the 1926–35 expedition with the help of one of the participants. In the remaining seven years of his life, Hedin published five books, three of them among the most important he had ever written.

First came the report on his own personal diplomacy during the war, entitled *Without Official Mission in Berlin,* published in 1949. It is a concise, well-written summary of Hedin's wartime journeys to Germany, based on voluminous entries in his diary and supplemented by documents that he kept in his personal archives. A year later, a massive, two-volume work appeared, totaling 1,000 pages and entitled *Great Men and Kings: Personal Memories of Sven Hedin.*

Of all of his books, this is without a doubt one of the most interesting. Through its pages passes a parade of great men—and two women—of three continents, Europe, America, and Asia. The book encompasses a long and busy lifetime, and it is a more candid and far less pretentious autobiography than those Hedin had written earlier. It is as if age gave him a different perspective: the author is still important, but he only represents the thread that binds this array of imposing and different personages together. The two volumes include glimpses of seventeen crown heads, one queen, and one president of the United States; leaders of Sweden, Denmark, Russia, Germany, Austria, Japan, Turkey, and Korea; and two popes, Pius XI and Pius XII.

The great explorers Hedin had met and in some cases known well start with Adolf Nordenskiöld, his childhood idol; there is Arminius Vámbéry, whose footsteps he followed in Iran; Nansen, Amundsen, and Robert Scott, all of polar fame; and Henry Stanley, the African traveler. The statesmen and generals, too, represent the great names of the late nineteenth and early twentieth century—Germans, Englishmen, Russians, Japanese, and one of Hedin's special heroes, Marshal Mannerheim of Finland.

The writers included in *Great Men and Kings* represent those Hedin admired rather than those he helped select as Nobel laureates in literature as a member of the Swedish Academy. Selma Lagerlöf, one of Sweden's most successful writers and a Nobel laureate, is the exception. Other portraits deal with the Nobel brothers, with Henry Ford, and with the German aircraft designer, Junkers. But only two geographers are included in Hedin's gallery of the famous: his master, Ferdinand von Richthofen, and one of the most unusual men in the history of the earth sciences, Prince Pyotr Kropotkin, Russian nobleman, anarchist, and geologist of great distinction.

The pages of *Great Men and Kings* display both Hedin's talents as a writer and his continuing concern with his own adventurous, exciting life, one in which each of these great personages played a part, even if it was only a walk-on that resulted in a cameo portrait.

One year after the publication of his massive biographical-autobiographical masterpiece, Hedin completed a second important political memoir, this one dealing with the Swedish defense crisis of 1912–14. It is, once again, a work that would do credit to a professional historian. It is fully documented, and it has become an important source on that critical period of Swedish history.

Hedin's last books, one published during his lifetime and one published the year after his death, dealt with his dogs and his horses in Asia. These were his companions during the early voyages before the First World War, and he describes them with affection and credits them with their share in his trials and triumphs. He did not, obviously, feel it necessary to write a book about the many Asians—camel drivers, cooks, scouts—who also served him faithfully during his expeditions. He must have believed that the words he used to portray and praise them in his earlier books did them full justice.

By itself, the literary productivity of Sven Hedin in his eighties would be surprising. When one adds to it several thousand pages of his diary, in which he described events in his own life and recorded and commented on the news of the day in the world at large, the sum of his work is truly astonishing.

Part of the explanation of Hedin's productivity lies in the fact that, in the words of his grandnephew, "he never rewrote anything. He never went over his manuscripts. That was the finished work" (Gösta Wetterlind, personal communication with author, 1974).

Another part was his lifestyle at home, where he did most of his writing. He worked at night, when he was least likely to be disturbed. He rose shortly before noon, received visitors during the afternoon, and after the evening meal retired to his study. The apartment he shared with his family occupied two floors; his library and living room were on the upper floor. At around eleven o'clock at night tea was served there, and for family and close friends that was the high point of the day. Hedin loved to tell stories, and his friends, for the most part, loved to listen.

Eric Wennerholm tells of an evening when Hedin had invited two close friends to his home, Carl Milles, the sculptor, and Anders de Wahl, one of the great Swedish actors of the time. Wennerholm, curious about how these three great men, all of them highly conscious of their importance, had passed an evening together, asked each of them in turn about the party. Milles said:

> Well, you know Hedin gave a lecture on his expeditions, and about the danger from Russia, and how a strong Germany was Europe's only salvation, you know, the sort of thing one hears these days. De Wahl was very trying, he insisted on reading part of one of his famous roles. But I must admit that both of them were enthusiastic about my idea of a statue to Tegnér, the poet.

Next, Wennerholm asked de Wahl, the actor, who said:

> Oh well, you know how it is at Hedin's. He kept harping on the same subject. But Milles was positively the worst. He talked about his years of poverty as a young artist in Paris, and every time you hear that story, he gets poorer and still poorer. But I read part of my famous current role, and they both insisted on hearing all of it.

Finally it was Hedin's turn to be asked about the meeting of the three great men. Hedin sighed:

> Well, I listened and listened, de Wahl and Milles kept talking big. In fact, you could hardly get a word in edgewise, until I started talking about Tibet, then they wanted to hear even more about that. Besides, neither of them understands politics. (Wennerholm 1978, 278–79)

The 1940s were difficult years for Hedin, not only because of the war that involved Germany but because of his own personal problem, his eyesight. He had had very little sight in one eye since his youth, and his good eye suddenly started to deteriorate. Between 1940 and 1949 he was nearly blind, and he walked with difficulty. Yet he continued to write every night. Finally his doctors persuaded him that although he was eighty-four years old, an operation to remove cataracts from his eyes was very likely to succeed. In June, 1949, he underwent the operation, and suddenly his eyesight returned to both eyes. When he returned home from the hospital, he looked at his sisters and exclaimed, "My, but you do look terribly wrinkled! Let me look in the mirror. Alas, I do, too" (Wennerholm 1978, 273). For the first time in sixty years, he had full vision in his left eye.

When the Second World War ended, Hedin felt very much alone in Sweden. Other Swedes had been sympathetic to Germany, but none had displayed that sympathy more openly than Hedin. When King Gustav V died in 1950, many people who knew the king were interviewed by the Swedish press. Hedin wrote bitterly in his diary: "No newspaper interviewed me, even though I had important things in common with the King; not one word about my chapter on Gustav V in *Great Men and Kings*, that appeared only a few weeks before his death!" (October 30, 1950). Slowly, however, people began to relent in their resentment of Hedin's pro-German attitudes.

On April 24, 1950, Vega Day in Sweden, Hedin was present at the formal dinner honoring Nordenskiöld. The president of the Swedish Geographical Society, host for the evening, welcomed the society's oldest honorary member, "who received his Vega Medal 52 years ago, and still honors the Society with his presence" (Diary, April 24, 1950). And in 1952, a few months before his death, Hedin again attended the Vega Day dinner. He spoke about his memories, having been invited to do so by King Gustav VI Adolf, who was present on the occasion.

Hedin felt ostracized by some of his countrymen because of his pro-German attitude. But that did not stop the steady stream of visitors who came to call at his home. "Our home is wonderful,"

145

he wrote in his diary in 1951, "it is an open *salon*, a caravanserai where people come from east and west. It certainly is not the quiet dwelling of a hermit" (March 24, 1951). On his eighty-fifth birthday, a year earlier, he had received 750 letters and 277 telegrams (Diary, February 26, 1950). He was not forgotten by his friends.

One message on that birthday came from a man Hedin admired more than most others he had known, Marshal Gustav Mannerheim. It read: "To my friend, a giant among explorers, my belated heartfelt wishes. May you spend many an eventful year in the newly-found light of your eyes!" (Mannerheim, February 19, 1950, Hedin Archives).

Though slowed down by recurring pain in his legs, Hedin continued to work at the same pace as before. His memory never faltered. In 1947, he spoke at the Swedish Academy of Sciences about the work of his friend and associate Erik Norin on the geology of western Tibet. He spoke for forty minutes without notes and drew sketch maps on the blackboard to illustrate his points (Diary, May 28, 1947).

One day in those last years, reminiscing about his travels, he said to his friend and lawyer Wennerholm:

> I feel as if I was standing on the borderline between two epochs, belonging to both. After the age of the saddle I was also part of the age of the automobile. And I witnessed how airplanes were put in the service of geographic research. (Wennerholm 1978, 254)

On August 7, 1952, Hedin and his family made a pilgrimage to the small country cemetery near Stockholm where his great-great-grandfather was buried. Sven Anders Hedin, after whom the explorer was named, had served the royal house of Sweden as personal physician of King Gustav III, thus laying the foundations of the close relationship that bound Hedin to the royal family throughout his life.

The entries in Hedin's diary grew shorter as the year 1952 drew on, from summer to fall. He no longer recorded and commented on daily events he heard about on the radio, but he continued to refer to visitors, to his family, and, occasionally, to his own health. On November 24, he did not get up at all. The family physician diagnosed a viral infection and prescribed medication. The next day he became unconscious, and he died early in the morning of November 26, 1952.

Four days before he died, Hedin wrote a longhand letter to a fifteen-year-old girl, daughter of a friend of Nils Ambolt, one of the members of the Sino-Swedish Expedition. The girl's teacher had asked her to speak to the class at school on Hedin's travels in Asia, and she was worried about doing well on her assignment.

Dear little Kajsa Stina Wickman,

Our common friend Nils Ambolt asked me to send you my picture and a few words, to prove that I am still alive, although it is the eighty-eighth winter that is now about to descend over my greying head.

I understand that you will speak at school about my travels in Asia. Greet the deserts and the mountains when you speak to them and tell them that I do not long after them any more, partly because of my old age, partly because of the wall of copper that the Reds in Russia and China built around the land of my youthful adventures that I love so much.

You and your classmates will, as you grow up, know infinitely more about Lake Lop-Nor, about the two-thousand year old ruins of cities, and about sacred Tibet than I did in my travels. But by that time I will have long since left this earth, and will dwell in a holier land, under the protection of God.

I do hope, however, that you shall report some of the amusing episodes from the time when I felt I was the sole ruler and sovereign of the heart of the largest continent of this earth.

With hearty greetings, your friend Sven Hedin. (November 22, 1952, Hedin Archives)

Less than one month before he died, Sven Hedin had signed his will, disposing of his possessions. The opening paragraph of the will sums up his outlook on his own career.

147

In view of the interest and support that I received in my life both from public and private sources, it is my wish that the materials I collected during my work be accessible to all and to continuing research. For that reason I declare, first, that what is presently in my study or deposited elsewhere, such as the Museum of Ethnography [in Stockholm], including books, notes, manuscripts, archives of correspondence, and a large number of maps, over 2,000 of my drawings, etc., shall be the property of the Royal Academy of Sciences, acting on behalf of the Museum of Ethnography. These collections will be the basis of a foundation, to be called the Sven Hedin Foundation, to be made available for research. . . . (Hedin Archives)

The printed books of Sven Hedin total some 30,000 pages; 3,200 of those are the result of work he did after his eightieth birthday. Hedin's Swiss biographer, Willy Hess, published the preliminary results of his investigations in a 130-page book. The items listed there—books, pamphlets, and published speeches— total nearly 900 (Hess 1962).

What was the judgment of his peers on Hedin's work? The prestigious Swedish journal *Geografiska Annaler* published a volume of 668 pages on Hedin's seventieth birthday in 1935. The volume is dedicated

to Sven Hedin on his 70th birthday, February 19, 1935. This tribute is offered as an expression of thanks for the devoted, indefatigable and successful work of a lifetime, devoted to the exploration of the largest continent of this earth, for the benefit of geographical research, and to the glory of the land and people of Sweden, by the Swedish Society for Anthropology and Geography. (*Hyllningsskrift* 1935)

The sixty-six essays that make up the memorial volume were contributed by scholars from Sweden, Germany, Austria, Switzerland, Denmark, Britain, France, the United States, and the Soviet Union.

Hedin's life bridged two centuries, and his life's work filled many books. The memorial volume offered to him by his colleagues in 1935 was a tribute to his skill as a scholar. Five years after his death, his successor in the Swedish Academy, Sten Selander, published the first volume of what was planned as a multivolume biography of Sven Hedin, who, next to Alfred Nobel, was the best-known Swede of his time. Selander's death prevented the completion of his project, but the first volume was considered so important that it was reviewed in a leading Stockholm daily newspaper, *Svenska Dagbladet*, by the dean of Swedish geographers, Professor Hans W:son Ahlmann.

Ahlmann and Hedin had disagreed on matters political and, at times, on scientific matters, too. Yet the review praises not only what is an outstanding portrait of Hedin's early career, but Hedin himself, the man and the scientist. The title of the review, "The Swedish Aladdin," is a clear reference to Hedin's extraordinary skill as a storyteller, his gift of evoking the spirit of people and places.

Ahlmann spoke of Hedin's extraordinary command of languages, his unlimited memory that never failed him, his phenomenal capability for work. The core of all his work, Ahlmann wrote, was his passion for maps. His mapmaking skills were extraordinary, as was his skill for making drawings of people, animals, and landscapes that often reached a high artistic level.

In 1904 a chair of geography had been created at the University of Stockholm with the hope that Hedin would accept the call to teach. He declined, partly because he did not believe he would adjust to the university life and partly because he believed that the tasks he set for himself demanded all his time and energy. Sven Hedin, in Ahlmann's words, undertook the mapping of some of the last blank areas left on the map in the Old World. For that reason alone, his is a place of honor among geographers. He will be remembered, wrote Ahlmann, "as a good and generous friend, a fine draftsman, a brilliant writer of his adventures in the service of science" (Ahlmann 1937).

It is a fitting thing that Hedin's name is still on the map of the city he loved most next to his native Stockholm, Berlin: in the Zehlendorf district of West Berlin there is a Sven Hedin Street and a Sven Hedin Square.

While the Second World War was raging over most of Europe, Hedin kept writing in the peace and quiet of neutral Sweden, evoking his beloved Inner Asia. The concluding paragraph of his *Reports from the Scientific Expedition to the Northwestern Provinces of China* summed up his own memories.

Everything is sunk in peace. But from the distance comes the scarcely audible sound of bells. I listen and as the minutes pass it grows more distinct. Now it is quite close at hand. Innumerable times before I have heard this sound in the eternal melody of the desert; but I cannot resist the desire to contemplate the regal gait of the camels. With slow, regular strides the caravan passes by, and the last camel in each string bears around its neck a bronze bell, whose heavy clapper gives tongue with every stride. Silent as shadows, the Chinese camel-men walk at the head of each string. The last camel, with an alert rider between his humps, strides past. Gradually the clang of bells dies away and silence spreads its wings over the earth again. (1937–, 25:312)

Bibliography

Works by Sven Hedin

Genom Persien, Mesopotamien och Kaukasien—Reseminnen (Across Persia, Mesopotamia and the Caucasus: Travel memories). Stockholm, 1887.

Konung Oscars beskickning till schahen af Persien år 1890 (King Oscar's embassy to the Shah of Persia in 1890). Stockholm, 1891.

"Der Demavend nach eigener Beobachtung" (Mount Demavend as seen through my observations). *Verhandlungen der Gesellschaft für Erdkunde zu Berlin* 19 (1892): 304–32.

Genom Khorasan och Turkestan (Across Khorasan and Turkestan). 2 vols. Stockholm, 1892–93.

Through Asia. 2 vols. London, 1898.

"Die geographisch-wissenschaftliche Ergebnisse meiner Reisen in Zentralasien, 1894–97" (The geographic and scientific results of my travels in Central Asia, 1894–97). *Petermanns Mitteilungen, Ergänzungsheft* 131 (1900). 399 pp., 6 maps.

Central Asia and Tibet: Towards the Holy City of Lassa. London, 1903.

Scientific Results of a Journey in Central Asia, 1899–1902. 6 vols. Stockholm, 1904–7.

Transhimalaya: Discoveries and Adventures in Tibet. 3 vols. London, 1909–13.

Overland to India. 2 vols. London, 1910.

Från pol till pol (From the North to the South Pole). 2 vols. Stockholm, 1911.

Ett varningsord (A warning). Stockholm, 1912.

Andra varningen (A second warning). Stockholm, 1913.

Från fronten i väster (From the western front). 2 vols. Stockholm, 1915.

Kriget mot Ryssland (War against Russia). Stockholm, 1915.

Till Jerusalem (To Jerusalem). Stockholm, 1917.

Bagdad, Babylon, Ninive. Leipzig, 1918.

Southern Tibet: Discoveries in Former Times Compared with My Own Researches. 9 vols. Stockholm, 1917–22.

Eine Routenaufnahme durch Ostpersien (A route survey across Eastern Persia). 2 vols. Stockholm, 1918–27.

En Levnads Teckning (Drawings of a lifetime). Stockholm, 1920.
Tsangpo Lamas vallfärd (The pilgrimage of Tsangpo Lama). 2 vols. Stockholm, 1920–22.
Resare-Bengt (Bengt the traveler). Stockholm, 1921.
Från Peking till Moskva (From Peking to Moscow). Stockholm, 1924.
Åter till Asien (Across the Gobi Desert). Stockholm, 1928.
Gobiöknens gåtor (Riddles of the Gobi Desert). Stockholm, 1930.
Mitt liv som upptäcktsresande (My life as an explorer). Stockholm, 1930.
Jehol, Kejserstaden (Jehol, the Imperial City). Stockholm, 1931.
Meister und Schüler: Ferdinand Freiherr von Richthofen an Sven Hedin (Master and student: Baron Ferdinand von Richthofen and Sven Hedin). Berlin, 1933.
Stora Hästens Flykt (The flight of the big horse). Stockholm, 1935.
Sidenvägen (The silk road). Stockholm, 1936.
Tyskland och Världsfreden (Germany and world peace). Stockholm, 1937.
Reports from the Scientific Expedition to the North-Western Province of China, under the Leadership of Dr. Sven Hedin. 54 vols. Stockholm, 1937–.
Sven Hedin und Albert Brockhaus: Eine Freundschaft in Briefen zwischen Autor und Verleger (Sven Hedin and Albert Brockhaus: letters in friendship between author and publisher). Leipzig, 1942.
Amerika i kontinenternas kamp (America in the struggle between continents). Stockholm, 1944.
Utan uppdrag i Berlin (On unofficial mission in Berlin). Stockholm, 1949.
Stormän och Kungar (Great men and kings). 2 vols. Stockholm, 1950.
Försvarsstriden, 1912–1914 (The issue of national defense, 1912–1914). Stockholm, 1951.
Mina hundar i Asien (My dogs in Asia). Stockholm, 1952.
Karavan och tarantass: Med hästar genom Asien (Caravan and tarantass: on horseback across Asia). Stockholm, 1953.

Works about Sven Hedin

Ahlmann, Hans W:son. "Den svenska Aladdin." *Svenska Dagbladet,* October 25, 1937.
Curzon, George Nathaniel, Lord. "Scientific Results of Dr. Sven Hedin's Expedition." *Geographical Journal* 33 (1909): 435–36.
Essén, Rütger. *Sven Hedin, ein grosses Leben.* Leoni, 1959.
Hedin, Alma. *Mein Bruder Sven.* Leipzig, 1925.
―――. *I Minnets Blomstergården* (In the garden of memory). Stockholm, 1950.
Hess, Willy. *Die Werke Sven Hedins. Versuch eines vollständigen Verzeichnisses.* (The works of Sven Hedin, an attempt at a complete listing). Vol. 1 of *Sven Hedin—Life and Letters.* Stockholm, 1962. A mimeo-

graphed supplement, *Erster Nachtrag* (First supplement), appeared in Stockholm, 1965.

Holdich, Sir Thomas. "Sven Hedin and Dutreuil de Rhins in Central Asia." *Geographical Journal* 13 (1899): 159–166.

Holm, Nils F. "Sven Hedins arkiv." *Svenska Arkivsamfundets skriftserie,* no. 16 (1974).

Hyllningsskrift tillägnad Sven Hedin (A volume of tributes offered to Sven Hedin). *Geografiska Annaler* 17 (1935).

Kohlenberg, Karl F. *Sven Hedin—Vorstoss nach Innerasien.* Balve-Sauerland, 1976.

de Margerie, Emmanuel. *L'oeuvre de Sven Hedin et l'orographie du Tibet.* Paris, 1929.

Montell, Gösta. "Sven Hedin the Explorer." *Geografiska Annaler* 36 (1954): 1–8.

Norin, Erik. "Sven Hedins Forskningsresor i Centralasien och Tibet." *Geografiska Annaler* 36 (1954): 9–39.

Ossian-Nilsson, Karl Gustaf. *Sven Hedin, Nobleman.* London, 1917.

Selander, Sten. *Sven Hedin—en äventrysberättelse.* Stockholm, 1957.

Wegener, Georg. "Das künstlerische in Sven Hedin." In *Hyllningsskrift tillägnad Sven Hedin. Geografiska Annaler* 17 (1935): 462–69.

Wennerholm, Eric. *Sven Hedin—en biografi.* Stockholm, 1978.

Other Sources

Carlgren, Wilhelm. *Sveriges utrikespolitik, 1939–1945.* Stockholm, 1973.

Gihl, Torsten. *Den svenska utrikenspolitikens historia.* Vol. 4, *1914–1919.* Stockholm, 1968.

Rennell Rodd, James. *Social and Diplomatic Memories.* 3d ser., *1902–1919.* London, 1925.

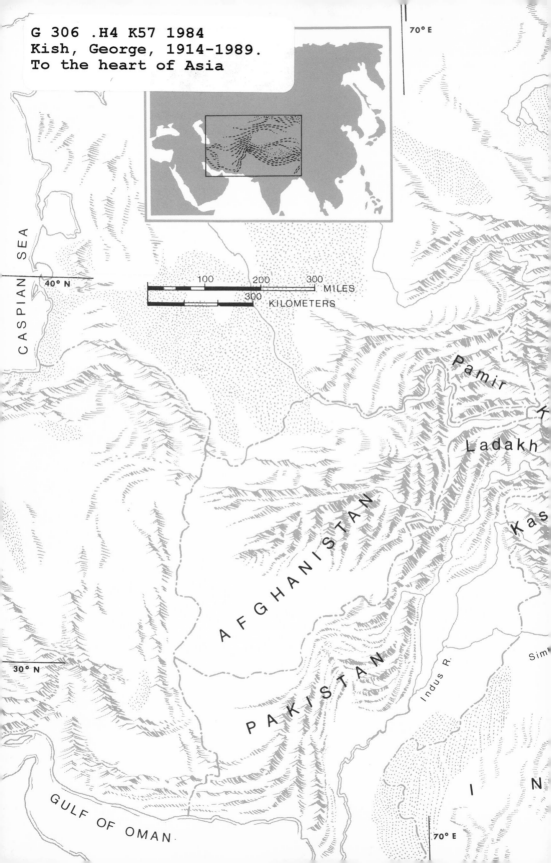

70° E

CASPIAN SEA

40° N

100   200   300
                                    MILES
        300
              KILOMETERS

30° N

Pamir

Ladakh

Kas

A F G H A N I S T A N

P A K I S T A N

Indus R.

Sim

GULF OF OMAN

I N

70° E